promo·art

RotoVision

Innovation in Invitations, Greetings, and Business Cards

Charlotte Rivers

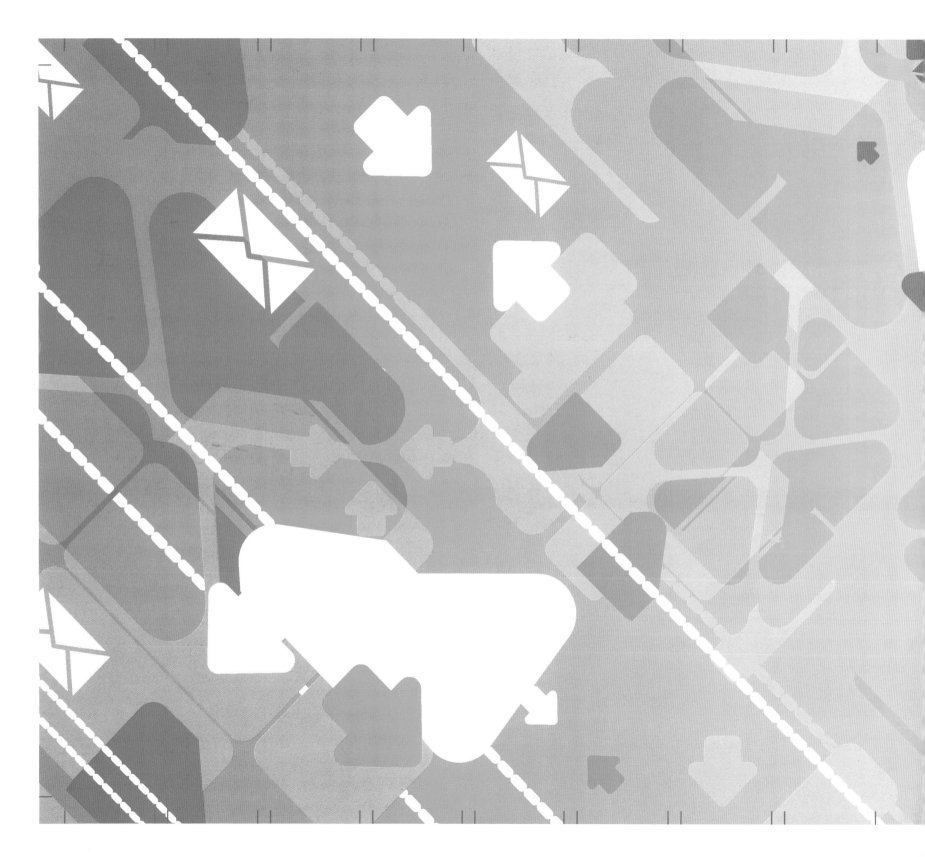

D

Books are to be returned on or before
the last date below.

31 OCT 2011

3·5·13

LIBREX-

promo-art

Innovation in Invitations, Greetings, and Business Cards

Charlotte Rivers

A RotoVision Book

Published and distributed by RotoVision SA
Route Suisse 9
CH-1295 Mies
Switzerland

RotoVision SA
Sales and Editorial Office
Sheridan House, 114 Western Road
Hove BN3 1DD, UK

Tel: +44 (0)1273 72 72 68
Fax: +44 (0)1273 72 72 69
www.rotovision.com

10 9 8 7 6 5 4 3 2 1

ISBN: 978-2-940361-95-3

Art Director: Jane Waterhouse
Design: Simon Slater, www.laki139.com
Photography: Simon Punter

Reprographics in Singapore by ProVision Pte.
Tel: +65 6334 7720 Fax: +65 6334 7721

Printed in China by Midas Printing International Ltd.

Contents

01

"The invitation is the ambassador. It needs to communicate something of the occasion or the company that it is announcing/representing."

Chris Turnbull, UK

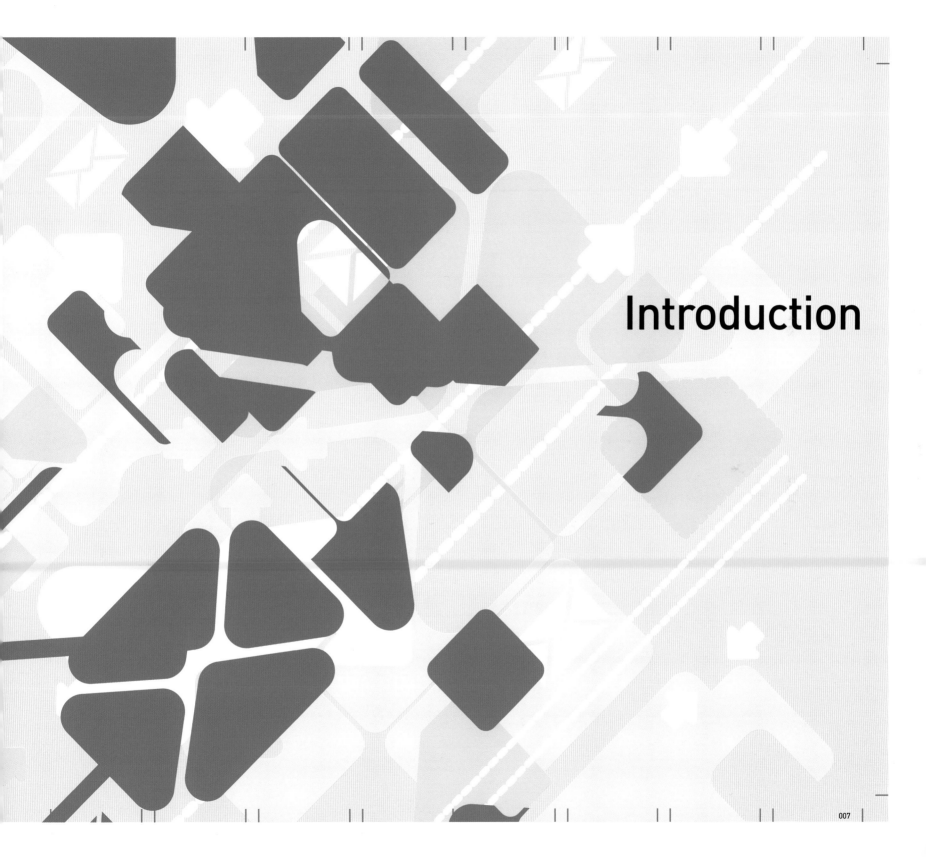

Introduction

From business cards and greetings cards to invitations and postcards, Promo-Art considers the many and varied ways in which designers choose to present themselves and their clients to the outside world. It looks at a wide range of global examples of promotional items that have been created via the medium of 2D print design, including examples of illustrators promoting their work through postcards, and designers wishing their clients a happy new year with greetings cards.

The idea of presenting yourself as a company and promoting your services has been around for years, but today creating promotional items, which are unique, stand-out, and, of course, represent the company they have been designed for, has become a top priority of any designer, whether working for themselves or for an independent client. This is what Promo-Art explores—the many different ways in which such items can be designed and realized. However, this book is not just about promotional items in the traditional sense—it also considers the design and creation of other cards, including wedding invitations and greetings cards.

Promo-Art has been divided into three main areas of focus: Artwork, Typography, and Printing and Finishing. Firstly, Artwork looks at the use of illustration and photography within the design of cards in all their formats, and explores the different ways in which designers work with both media to interesting effect. Both forms of artwork bring unique character to the cards on which they are used. Whether it is through having an image of a person on their own business card, or through using an illustration on a wedding invitation, there are some great examples of how the experimental use of artwork can set a card apart, challenging the design norm.

One of my personal favorites is Liam Johnstone's series of business cards. He created a Noah's Ark image, which he printed on one side of a sheet, with his business card in two columns of five on the other side. The Noah's Ark image can only be realized again once all ten business cards are laid out together. Clara Courtaigne and Richard Monk created a series of cards that ask the recipient to do the work and create the imagery themselves in their Dotty for You greetings cards. The idea is that the recipient must draw on the card to complete it and reveal the message that they have been sent. Whatever the card, together all the examples in the Artwork chapter demonstrate how creative use of imagery in all its forms can bring a piece of design to life.

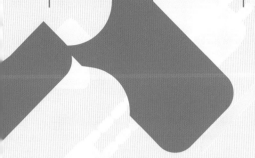

Typography covers the typographic design and layouts employed by designers to inform and communicate. It looks at the different ways in which type can be used as both image and text to convey information to the viewer. There is Underline Studio's holiday greeting and moving card, which lists the street name of each person/company it was sent to around the world. Each one has been personalized by the use of a single "underline" under the street name of each individual/company that it was sent to—an interesting typography-based idea that has been cleverly executed.

Finally, the Printing & Finishing chapter looks at the huge variety of stocks, inks, printing techniques, and finishes used by designers to differentiate an item, giving it a unique tactile quality or special finish. It is through pushing the boundaries of print production techniques that a flat, 2D design can really come alive. Even on a limited budget, there are simple, inexpensive ways to make a print design job stand out. Designers can experiment with the materials, or manipulation of the stock they are working with, and the opportunities are many, varied, and ever-growing. For example, Radford Wallis used debossed silver "turkey" foil to create its company Christmas card, and Peter and Paul created a business card using old vinyl records. Such experimentation is not always possible, or practical, but should the brief allow, the use of different materials and inks can add great character and individuality to a design and help to give a card stand-out.

As with all the books in the –Art series, Promo-Art looks at a global selection of innovative graphic design with the aim of providing design inspiration. Enjoy!

Charlotte Rivers

02

"All communication design needs to appeal to one aspect of human interest or another—be it visual or intellectual, or a combination of the two."

Peter Crnokrak, UK

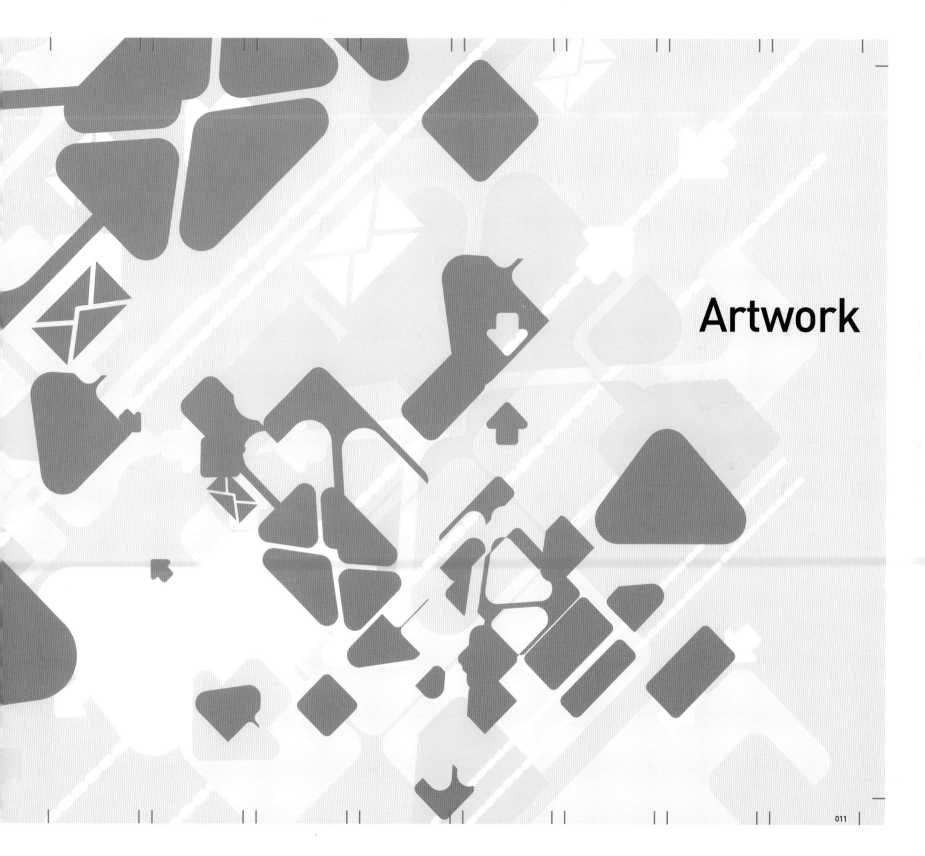

Artwork

Introduction

Whether they use illustration or photography, cards in all their formats offer a great opportunity to experiment with artwork. Both forms of artwork bring unique character to the cards on which they are used. Throughout this chapter we see how designers have experimented with artwork in many different ways. There are examples of work featuring photography, Lomography, and various illustrative styles.

"Exhibition invitations are always nice to do, as you can treat them as a further piece of artwork within the show."

Ariel Aguilera and Andrea Benyi, Australia/Germany

Client: **Clara Courtaigne**
Design: **Clara Courtaigne**
Photography: **Clara Courtaigne**
Country: **UK**

I Send You Buttons Because Flowers Die postcards

"I always feel sad offering flowers to people, as they are perishable," explains Courtaigne. "This set of postcards was my first attempt to resolve this problem, and it also refers to a famous song by Jacques Brel, a Belgian singer, who wrote a song entitled 'I brought you sweets because flowers are perishable.'" The card images come from a set of pictures that Courtaigne took in Regent's Park, London. She placed different kinds of buttons, previously bought in a flea market in Paris, in the tree blossom around the park. On the cards' reverse, there are images of a different family of buttons in flowerpots. Images of the buttons as they were originally bought—attached to card—have been used to indicate where the stamp should be affixed on the card.

Client: **310k**
Design: **Ivo Schmetz/Paul Rickus at 310k**
Country: **The Netherlands**

310k business cards

Schmetz and Rickus designed these cards for themselves. They share a love of graphic design and snowboarding, so they used images of themselves in their snowboard gear in front of the mountains on their business cards. However, the mountains are not real, Rickus' card has a picture of Schmetz, and Schmetz's card a picture of Rickus. "The idea behind this is that if you give your business card to someone you've met, they have seen you, but they might not have seen the other member of 310k—so when they get the card, they have in a way met the whole company," explains Schmetz. Chicago typeface is used on the cards, which have been printed in CMYK with a dot of fluorescent orange.

310k
paul rickus
me@310k.nl
+31(0)614663774

www.310k.nl

310k
ivo schmetz
we@310k.nl
+31 (0)6 22616985

www.310k.nl

Client: **Haven Licensing**
Design: **Deuce Design**
Country: **Australia**

Haven Licensing business cards

"The main idea behind the cards is that they show the Haven stable of brands in a unique way," explains Maggie Tang at Deuce Design. "Each director has ten different cards; every card features a spontaneous snapshot of the product with a consumer." Deuce Design shot the pictures with Lomo cameras over a three-month period, and used over 500 different pieces of entertainment products and plush toys. The idea was for the photography to be natural and candid, and to feature real life models. Helvetica Rounded typeface has been used throughout. The series has fostered a "collect all ten" mindset.

Client: **Platform Artist Group Inc.**
Design: **Ariel Aguilera at Pandarosa**
Country: **Australia**

Secret Shelf Life of Us invitation

Platform, a public art gallery, exhibits works within cabinets situated on the subway of Melbourne's central train station. Pandarosa designed this invite for a show called Secret Shelf Life of Us, curated by the gallery. The show's title inspired Pandarosa to use photographs of the shelves in its studio on the invite. "The idea was to show the different aspects/inspirations/things we collect and which we then keep on our shelves and how that is a representation of what we are and the tastes we have," explains Aguilera. Each artist created and presented a piece of work within the cabinet using some kind of shelving unit.

Client: **pleaseletmedesign**
Design: **Damien Aresta at pleaseletmedesign**
Photography: **Olivier Cornil**
Countries: **Belgium/Luxembourg**

pleaseletmedesign business cards

pleaseletmedesign designed these two different sets of business cards for its own use. It created the necktie cards using pictures of its partners that were originally made for an exhibition. "These photographs were perfect for what we wanted to show on our business cards: no faces, but a certain idea of making good images, seriously," explains Aresta. "Then, following the concept of our collection of prints we had created that displayed their own denomination— there were posters, T-shirts, badges, and stickers—we decided to make the business cards too." Franklin Gothic typeface was used for its simplicity.

BUSINESS CARD

PIERRE & DAMIEN, PLEASELETMEDESIGN
GRAPHIC DESIGN + EVERYTHING ELSE

11 AVENUE DU MONT KEMMEL
1190 BRUSSELS, BELGIUM

STUDIO +32 0 2 502 78 64
PIERRE +32 0 484 500 194
DAMIEN +32 0 485 688 297

OH@PLEASELETMEDESIGN.COM
WWW.PLEASELETMEDESIGN.COM

Client: **Oscar & Ewan**
Design: **Oscar & Ewan**
Country: **UK**

Oscar & Ewan
Christmas card

Oscar Bauer and Ewan Robertson designed this Christmas card. "It was designed to spread a bit of love and humor around Christmas time," explain Bauer and Robertson. "There is no type, therefore no send-off, just a card in the spirit of Christmas, and we think that at a time of commercialism people felt oddly surprised when they picked up a card with no selling point." Printed in an edition of 1,000, Bauer and Robertson distributed the cards by hand across London, including on buses, trains, and anywhere else they went over the Holiday period.

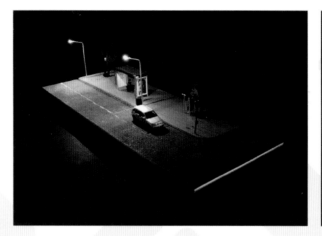

Client: **Context Department, Central Saint Martins College of Art & Design**
Design: **Oscar Bauer/Ewan Robertson/ Matt Bucknall/Jennie Hancock**
Country: **UK**

Context Collected invitation

This invite was designed for an exhibition of visual pieces from a major research project held at St Bride Printing Library by the Context Department at Central Saint Martins College of Art & Design, London. Bauer, Robertson, Bucknall, and Hancock went to St Bride, took pictures of its interior, and used them on the invite. "It's a beautiful room suspended in time," explains Bauer. "We complemented photos of the brown 1960s decor with neon-green tabs for the flier and posters, then used the tabs again as signage. We didn't want to change the space so we just applied something on top. We chose the neon green to get a fun sharp contrast and visual language." News Gothic typeface has been used throughout to add to the identity contrast.

Client: **Sugar Factory**
Design: **Ivo Schmetz at 310k**
Country: **The Netherlands**

Sugar Factory postcards

310k designed these postcards for the Sugar Factory, a club/night theater in central Amsterdam, to promote the venue and its program. 310k also designed the club's logo, house style, website, and other promotional items. "We were asked to make cards that would catch people's eye among the mountain of cards and fliers around Amsterdam, and we wanted them to be humorous too," says Schmetz. "Inspired by the venue's name, we thought of a simple idea—to create funny images with sugar—so we bought loads of sugar and started taking pictures of it." The result is a series of unusual and amusing pictorial postcards.

Client: **Ikon Gallery**
Design: **James Langdon**
Country: **UK**

Series of exhibition invitations

Each of these invitation cards announces an exhibition at Ikon Gallery, a major contemporary art space in Birmingham, UK. The invitation design concepts connect with and embody the gallery's programming approach, which consists almost exclusively of solo exhibitions with artists presenting a single large piece of work, or a body of work developed over time. A dedicated card is always made for each artist, even though often two or more exhibitions run concurrently. "Broadly speaking the series is intended to be simply designed with an emphasis on good reproductions of the artists' work, and a satisfying material quality,"

explains Langdon. "Within this, though, there are subtly different approaches being taken depending on the nature of the exhibition. For example, there are some cards where the image is at quite a tangent to the actual exhibition: a picture of work in the studio, a piece of research, or a site that is connected to the exhibition for example. Other cards are more graphic; this is often the case with new commissions, where the artwork doesn't exist at the time when the invitation is being prepared." The cards are typeset in Fedra Sans Alt with its clean forms complementing their simple presentation.

Client: **Oscar & Ewan**
Design: **Oscar & Ewan**
Country: **UK**

Oscar & Ewan business card

Oscar Bauer and Ewan Robertson created these business cards when they launched their own design agency. The card image is of an office, taken from a set the pair built for an advert competition for Kodak. "Sharing an office and a lot of work, Ewan and I decided to keep cost down and share one business card... It felt like a nice image and a fun twist on a design office," explains Bauer. As it was a joint business card with both their details, they took some of the cards and punched half a hole on the edge next to their own name before giving them out.

OSCAR & EWAN

332 Kingsland Road
London
E8 4DA

www.oscarandewan.co.uk
mail@oscarandewan.co.uk

OSCAR BAUER

+44 (0)7906 730 821
oscar@oscarandewan.co.uk

EWAN ROBERTSON

+44 (0)7929 645 272
ewan@oscarandewan.co.uk

Client: **Red Design**
Design: **Red Design**
Country: **UK**

Red Design Christmas card/mailer

Red Design created this Christmas card/mailer to send to its existing and potential clients. As it is interested in the questions surrounding sustainability of design, it wanted to create a card/mailer that had minimum impact on the environment in terms of materials and processes. The result is a series of cards that have been created using secondhand postcards sourced from junk shops. Bold bespoke type containing the company information and Christmas message has then been screenprinted over the images. This process reappropriates the original image, marking it as a piece of design, as well as creating something new from the old.

Illustration

"I've spent my life drawing in some capacity;
I think an illustrative element can add
another layer and dimension."

Bruce Slorach, Australia

Client: **KYN**
Design: **Pandarosa**
Country: **Australia**

KYN playing cards

Pandarosa designed these playing cards for the launch of wine label KYN. "We were asked to create a set of playing cards using the illustrative characters featured on the wine label," explains Ariel Aguilera. "We created a Jack, Queen, King, and Joker using the characters of an owl, fox, rabbit, and cat." The card sets were sent to various media and handed out at the launch. The storytelling theme was carried out throughout all parts of the brand; even the wine labels on the back of the bottle featured various Golden Book–style stories, which were also used in the card set as separate cards. The choice of a playing-card set came about from the idea of an interactive experience in which the audience could engage and then maybe create its own form of storytelling.

Client: **Scott Hardkiss/Stephanie Diaz-Matos**
Design: **Tatiana Arocha**
Country: **USA**

Amor Vincit Omnia wedding invitation

Arocha designed this invitation for the wedding of Scott Hardkiss and Stephanie Diaz-Matos. Both work in the music industry, Hardkiss as a DJ and producer, and Diaz-Matos as a music supervisor for movies and TV shows. "They liked my art a lot and they wanted me to do a piece for their wedding," explains Arocha. "They wanted to have lilies, and the artwork needed to be independent from the information; the theme was 'Amor Vincit Omnia.'" Arocha created imagery that combined two symbolic images for the couple; Diaz-Matos' favorite flower is the lily, and Hardkiss has used fish imagery in his past album covers. "I combined both elements as a symbol of their union," adds Arocha. Both images are from 18th-century books of botanical and animal engravings, with Arocha giving them a graphic treatment. Emily typeface was used, and the invite was printed on a letterpress with gold-foil accent. Each card was numbered as part of an edition.

Client: **Clara Courtaigne/Richard Monk**
Design: **Clara Courtaigne/Richard Monk**
Country: **UK**

A Thousand Words greetings cards

Courtaigne and Monk designed this set of greetings cards for Christmas, Valentine's Day, and birthdays. They wanted to create make-your-own cards that were both personal and fun. "We wanted to take the intimidation out of drawing and making a card for someone by encouraging the sender to have an idea and giving them the confidence to express it creatively," explains Courtaigne. "The basis for these make-your-own cards was to illustrate your love or friendship for someone. Each card carries the words, 'If it was possible I would give you ...' or 'This shows how big my love is for you ...' above an empty space to let the sender's imagination run riot." For inspiration a list of possible gifts was included, along with a series of stickers to get people started on their own *mise-en-scène*.

Client: **Studio Mielo**
Design: **Katharina Leuzinger**
   at **Studio Mielo**
Country: **UK**

Studio Mielo business cards

Leuzinger designed these business cards for her studio, Studio Mielo. The cards feature several different pencil and ink drawings that Leuzinger created on paper, scanned, and worked over using Photoshop. She has chosen to print the images in single color (black) onto gray card to make a series of simple, yet memorable business cards.

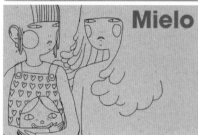

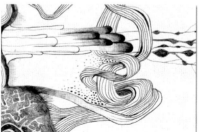

Client: **Christian Albriktsen**
Design: **Christian Albriktsen**
Country: **Norway**

Christian Albriktsen business cards

The imagery on these business cards forms part of a series of silhouette icons used on the different elements of Albriktsen's overall identity. "They represent things I'm interested in, things I like, and other stuff that I feel represents me." Albriksten drew the images himself and has used Avant Garde and Utopia typefaces. "I think Avant Garde has a little bit more presence than similar faces, but still retains a level of anonymity—and also I've always been into that retro kind of stuff." The cards are printed in one color, but on various-colored stock to give them more scope.

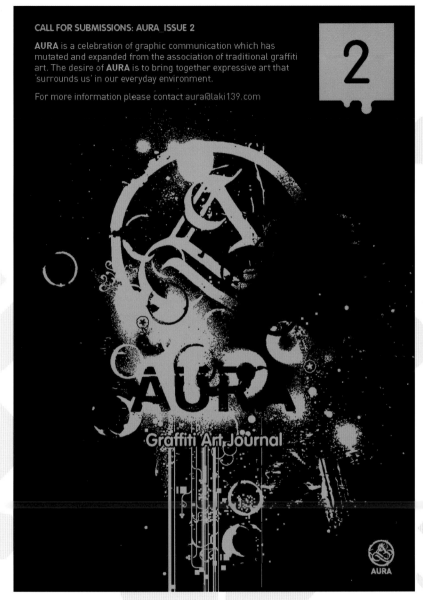

CALL FOR SUBMISSIONS: AURA_ISSUE 2

AURA is a celebration of graphic communication which has mutated and expanded from the association of traditional graffiti art. The desire of AURA is to bring together expressive art that 'surrounds us' in our everyday environment.

For more information please contact aura@laki139.com

Client: **AURA Graffiti Art Journal**
Design: **Simon Slater at LAKI 139**
Country: **UK**

AURA 2 call for submissions postcard

LAKI 139 produced this postcard to send out to prospective artists interested in contributing samples of their work for Issue 2 of <u>AURA Graffiti Art Journal</u>. The front includes a brief description of the journal. It also shows artwork created from the <u>AURA</u> logo. The back of the card shows spread samples, poster artwork, a packshot, and a description of Issue 1. The cards were printed on 400g matte stock with a matte laminate for durability.

Client: **Harms und Müller**
Design: **Sebastian Bagge/Julio Rölle**
    at **44flavours**
Country: **Germany**

Harms and Müller business card

44flavours designed the corporate identity (including the logo and these business cards) for garden architects Harms and Müller. "The main idea behind the design was to capture the feeling of the company and to create something a little different, something that had connotations of the extravagant, and something with a young spirit," explains Rölle. "The imagery we worked with on the cards includes all the items they use for their work, and we wanted them to create the feeling that the company is busy and active." Together the images create a pattern on the card background on which sits the company logo, like a family crest. The cards have been printed in two different colors, one for each partner.

Client: **Maldesign**
Design: **Andy Mallalieu at Maldesign**
Country: **UK**

Maldesign business card

The main aim of Mallalieu's business card, other than giving the usual contact details, was to convey his illustration style and design work. The front of the card features an illustration by Mallalieu, and the back is clean-cut and graphical with all type set in Helvetica. To finish, the card has been matte-laminated on both sides.

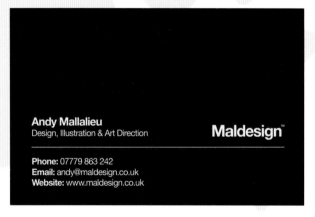

Client: **Little Oranges**
Design: **Emily Desai at Little Oranges**
Country: **USA**

Cal*LINE (Classic American Letterpress) greetings cards

Desai designed this series of cards as one of the company's signature card lines. "For this new line, we really wanted a man-friendly feel," explains Desai. "I am trained as an architect and wanted to design a line of cards that focus on minimal use of color and artwork, while clearly communicating the sentiment. A single chair with a cast shadow and the words 'Miss you' is one of the most popular cards in the line. For the 'feel' and inspiration of Cal*LINE, we wanted to reminisce on the California of John Steinbeck and also the minimal aesthetic of mid-century modernism in design and architecture." Each card features unique drawings, all originals and inspired by vintage furniture, windmills, telephone lines—somewhat generic images that are universal in nature. "We looked for solid images that worked with the expression of the card, for instance, our 'Drop me a Line' card features telephone wires—simple, but effective." The cards are letterpressed on an antique hand-fed machine with hand-mixed inks.

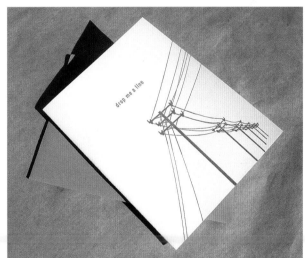

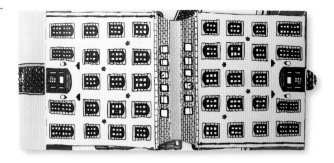

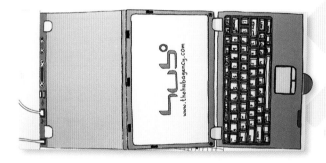

Client: **The Hub Agency**
Design: **Adam Smith Design**
Country: **UK**

The Hub Agency mailers

Smith designed these two 3D mailers
for the Hub Agency (a design, advertising,
and branding company) to promote the
launch of its new website. The mailer
had to be made from a single piece
of card. "The idea for the mechanics of
the cards came from a combination
of children's pop-up books and origami
paper art," explains Smith. "The mailer
was made to reflect the Hub Agency's
fresh, quirky side and also be memorable.
The idea was that these mailers would be
kept, and sit on the recipient's desk." The
images and typefaces were hand-drawn.

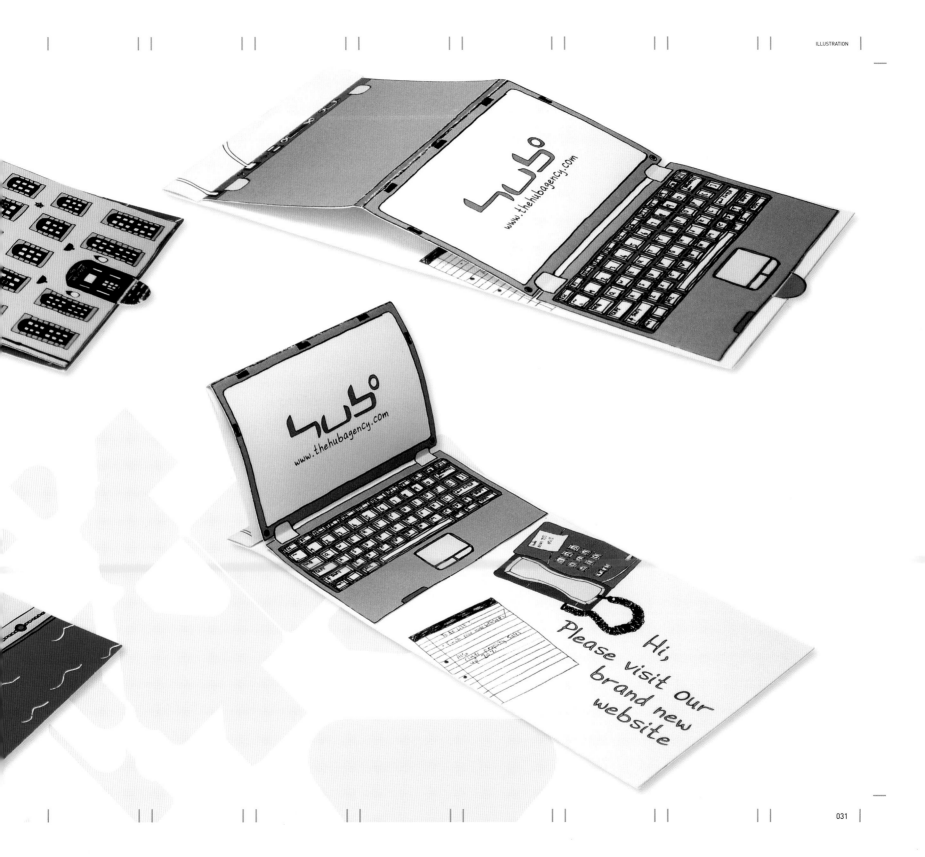

Client: **Julien Macdonald**
Design: **Steven Wilson**
Country: **UK**

Julien Macdonald
crest invitation

Wilson designed the invite for fashion designer Julien Macdonald "I had initially designed a floral fabric print for him that was used in his designs for that season, so he wanted to integrate the flowers into the invite design as well," explains Wilson. "It was Julien who suggested a crest. I guess he liked the idea of something regal, as his show is always a big event within London fashion week, and he wanted to play on the idea of that with a crest, something usually associated with high society, establishment, and of course royalty." Wilson has created a crest that contains horses, shields, initials, and flowers—fairly typical elements within a traditional crest, but given a more contemporary feel.

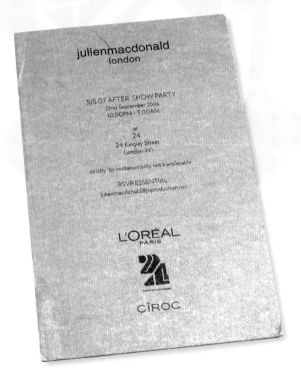

Client: **Studio Thomson/Major Players Recruitment Agency**
Design: **Katharina Leuzinger**
Country: **UK**

Rainbow Trust Children's Charity greetings cards

Leuzinger designed the cards as part of a collection from different artists and designers to raise money for the Rainbow Trust Children's Charity, a charity for children with a life-threatening or terminal illness. The project was launched jointly by design company Studio Thomson and design recruitment agency Major Players. They asked ten different designers and artists to supply their artwork free for this cause. "The idea behind the designs was that they should look friendly, happy, and positive," explains Leuzinger. "I also wanted to give the cards a certain childlike quality and simplicity. I created these designs that work as repeat patterns so they work as imaginary children's duvet covers or curtains inspired by my own childhood memories of bold and simple textile prints. The simplicity of the shapes and the bright colors express a soothing and positive feel. Even though the cards were not for the children themselves, I wanted to create something that would make them feel happy, looking at them."

Client: **Melanie Lane/Photone/Volker Schumacher/Sven Saatkamp**
Design: **Sebastian Bagge/Julio Rölle at 44flavours**
Country: **Germany**

Under Violent Objects invitation

Bagge and Rölle designed this invite for Under Violent Objects, a solo dance show by dancer Melanie Lane and visual sound duo Photone. The show questions the influence of media, social expectations, and cultural and political structure on society. It looks at one person's advance and struggle toward a peaceful existence. "We started by talking about the title of the show and looking through recent artwork we'd been working on," explains Rölle. "I did a couple of paintings/screen prints, inspired by photographs I'd taken in Brooklyn one summer that fit with the title, which in our opinion had a lot to do with observation and camera surveillance. We flipped the idea, imagined we were under public surveillance, and realized that if we were we would mask ourselves, which is why we created this imagery." Colorfarm typeface has been used.

Client: **Ryan Renshaw gallery**
Design: **Ariel Aguilera at Pandarosa**
Country: **Australia**

Monoe invitation

Pandarosa designed this invite for its solo show Monoe. It features a floral image based on a reinterpretation of some of the pieces of work created by Pandarosa and shown within the exhibition. "We wanted the invite to give a sense of the type of work we would be creating for the show," explains Aguilera. "This was done through the use of color, which was the same on the invite as it was in all the works in the exhibition." Pandarosa created all typefaces used on the invite.

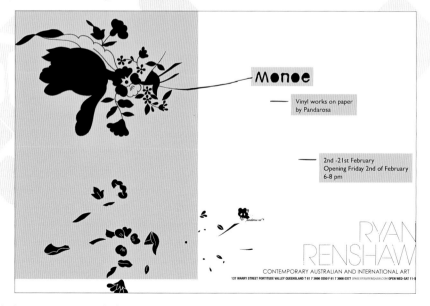

Client: **Private**
Design: **Studio Daniel Baer**
Country: **UK**

Wedding invitation and thank-you card

Baer designed this wedding invitation and thank-you card for a leading interiors stylist and editor so it would have the feel of a limited-edition piece of artwork, a piece of design that people would want to keep after the wedding celebration was over. The hand-drawn illustration on the cards is full of hidden symbols and has several different exotic flora and fauna; for instance, the heart in the middle has been created using "bleeding heart" flowers, which was also the name of the venue for the wedding reception. The negative shape of the illustration on the wedding invitation was used to print a thank-you card, which was sent out after the wedding. "The illustration is a personal interpretation of the celebration, and was designed as my gift to the bride and groom," explains Baer. Both pieces were hand screen-printed on heavy card.

Client: **Daniel Reisinger/Straighty 180**
Design: **Maggie Tang at Deuce Design**
Country: **Australia**

Straighty 180 business card

Deuce Design designed this business card for movie director Daniel Reisinger and his company Straighty 180. Its brief was to create a card that was unique, different, featured a jester, perhaps had a moving part, and something potential clients would remember and wouldn't discard. "He wanted the card to have a combination of many elements, including items that had a sense of mischief, playing-card influences, patterns," explains Tang. "The idea was about the deal, the game, a poker face, and all elements common to business and moviemaking." The card has a strong connection to a pack of playing cards. Its primary side has Reisinger's contact details and a spinning wheel, which has a cut-out that when spun reveals the words: truth, mischief, and beauty. This side also features a classic tribal repeat pattern. The reverse has the company identity and stencil-style jester illustration.

Client: **Adam Smith**
Design: **Adam Smith Design**
Country: **UK**

Low-Res mailers

Smith designed this series of retro computer models as promotional items to be sent with an invite to his degree show at the Edinburgh College of Art. He referred to images of the actual computers to create his hand-drawn versions. Each one was drawn on a single sheet of paper and then cut out with scissors, folded and assembled, and secured together with glue—a simple, yet effective method of production. "The idea behind creating these computers really came from a personal interest in the development of the computer over the years as an essential tool for design," explains Smith. One set of the computer models was sold to a client in the USA.

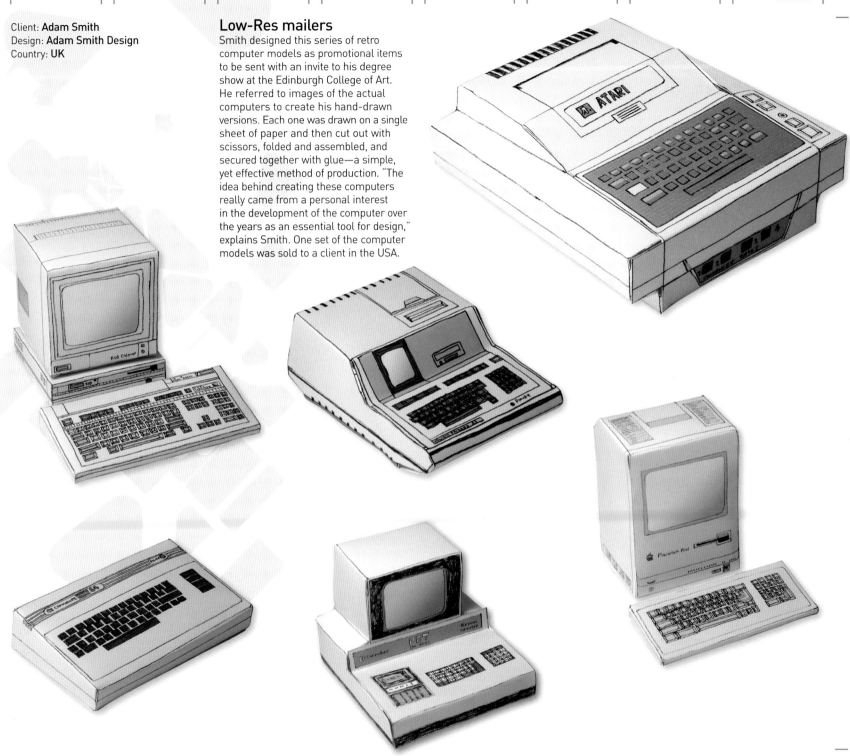

Client: Tatiana Arocha/Alex Moulton
Design: Tatiana Arocha
Country: USA

Tatiana Arocha & Alex Moulton wedding invitation

Arocha designed this invitation for her own wedding to Alex Moulton. "The wedding took place at my dad's house in Colombia and I wanted the imagery to be inspired by the gardens and nature that surround his house," explains Arocha, who drew the delicate flower illustrations. "I did this because I wanted something personal and very intimate." The illustration features on the front by itself, and on the reverse together with the details of the wedding. The text has been set in Berkeley typeface, which was chosen for its classic and elegant look, keeping it very legible. The invite was printed on a letterpress. Each card was numbered as part of an edition.

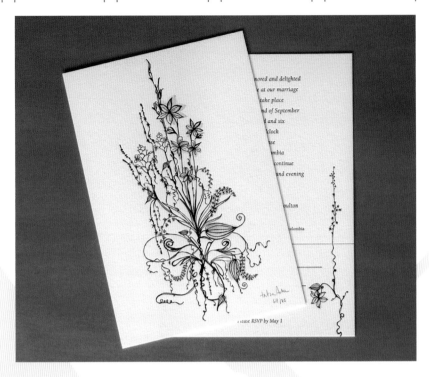

Client: IMP gallery
Design: Pandarosa
Country: Australia

Miscellany invitation

Pandarosa designed the invite for its solo show Miscellany. To give a sense of the diverse range of work created for the show (drawings, installation, mural, works on paper, 3D structures, and so on), the invite was created by collating a range of elements from work featured in the show to produce one single image. The collage/illustration is accompanied by a decorative hand-drawn typeface used for the exhibition title, with a traditional serif typeface for the remaining text.

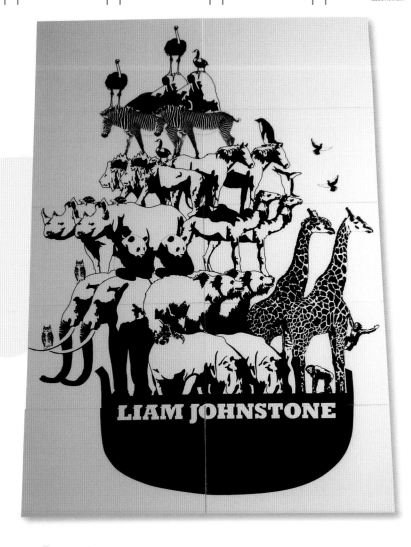

Client: **Liam Johnstone**
Design: **Liam Johnstone**
Country: **Canada**

Animals business cards

Johnstone created this series of ten business cards to promote himself as someone who is creative and really enjoys what he does. His idea began after he created the Noah's Ark illustration shown here, which is only realized when all ten cards are laid out together, reverse-side up, in the right order. "I really liked the idea of this little ark carrying the future, which I feel fits with my current position as a young designer," he adds.

"I've also always loved puns and idioms since I was a child, and sayings such as 'An elephant never forgets' have stuck out in my mind... I gathered as many of these sayings as I could and chose the ten most positive, including 'I'm smarter than the average bear' and 'I'm wise as an owl.'" Johnstone has applied the sayings, together with an illustration of the relevant animal or bird, on the front of the cards. The ten different cards have

been printed in two columns of five on a single sheet with the ark image printed on its reverse so when the cards are cut out, each one has a piece of the illustration. Franklin Gothic typeface has been used throughout.

Client: **The Arts Foundation**
Design: **Helen Crawford-White**
    at Crush Design
Country: **UK**

Arts Foundation invitation

The Arts Foundation is an independent
trust and its fellowship programme was
initiated to support individual artists who
have reached some professional standing
in their art form. This invite was created
for its 2007 awards event; it served as an
entry ticket and gave information about
the Arts Foundation's work, the five art
forms (glass, photojournalism, electro-
acoustic composition, new fiction, and
theater for children and young people),
and the shortlisted nominations. "The
idea was to focus on the five categories
for this year's event and bring these to
life using quirky illustrative type," explains
Crawford-White. "There are seven cards.
Five feature one of the categories, where
the word is illustrated using imagery
relating to that category, then there is
one card featuring information on the Arts
Foundation organization, and the last
card is the actual invite." Crawford-White
created the illustrations. The cards were
screenprinted in two colors on two
different colors of card.

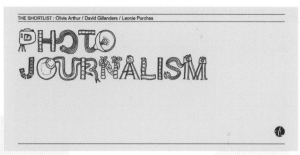

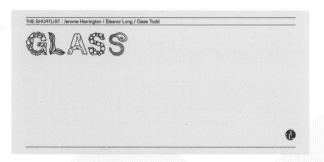

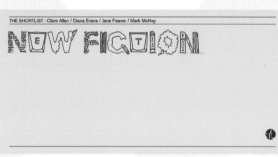

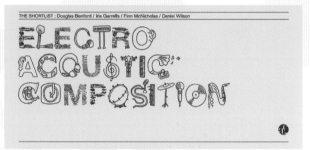

Client: **Nookart**
Design: **Katharina Leuzinger**
Countries: **Australia/UK**

Nookart greetings cards

Leuzinger designed these cards as part of a product range series for wholesale company Nookart. "The company is renowned for its 'cute' products," she explains, "so the brief was to make something sweet and cutesy. I chose simple shapes and color combinations to create the characters on the cards as I didn't want to end up with something kitsch." The cards were created as vector graphics in Illustrator. Designed to be screenprinted in a few inks onto gray card, for Nookart they were printed in a four-color process. They were sold in various stores and outlets in the USA, Europe, and Australia.

Client: **Les Enfants Terribles (LET)**
Design: **Jonas Hellström at Lobby Design**
Country: **Sweden**

LET Summer Party invitation

Lobby Design created this invitation for the Swedish culture magazine Les Enfants Terribles (LET) and its members' club, Club LET. "We had total freedom within the design, except that the invitations and all other parts had to have the vibe of summer," explains Hellström. "Inspiration came from all the life that the summer brings: the green leaves and the light from the sun, sunset, and growth."

Lobby Design scanned plants and branches, then traced the pictures using Streamline. The logo for the magazine is handmade and the typeface for Club LET is Helvetica.

Client: **Belinda, S. Chen**
Design: **Belinda, S. Chen**
Country: **UK**

Magic Brick Lane postcards

Chen created this series of illustrated cards for a college project. Her idea was to "discover the culture and atmosphere on this street" (Brick Lane in London). "I wanted to show the street in a different way, so it wasn't just about its history and multi-culturalism, I wanted the images to have a more playful sense, "explains Chen. "The images I've used on the postcards are from my sketchbook and then I've played with them to create these collage illustrations/images." Chen created the type by taking letters from different magazines, newspapers, and packaging.

Client: **City of Bath College**
Design: **Tom Rowe at Evening Tweed**
Country: **UK**

Welcome to the Hothouse invitation

Tom Rowe designed this invite for an end-of-year show at the City of Bath College, UK. Each year a different department designs the invite. Rowe and Pat Saville were asked to create an identity and subsequent material for the exhibition. Saville worked on the signage, labeling, and maps, and Rowe on the invites and posters. "We decided to focus the identity of the exhibition on the Gainsborough Building where the art department is situated," explains Rowe. "The building was unfortunately going to be sold off so we decided to celebrate the building's life by making it the focal point of the exhibition identity." Rowe has used a cut-and-paste style to create the invite, which features the use of many images of plants and foliage as a representation of the artists' creative juices flowing around and out of the building. The main title is set in Extra Ornamental with other copy in Hoefler.

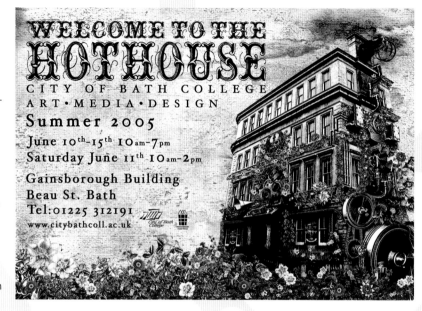

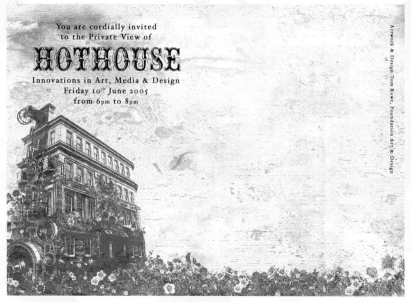

Artwork & Design Tom Rowe, Foundation Art & Design

Client: **Pari Bijarzahi**
Design: **Kristina Bowers**
Country: **UK**

Pari Bijarzahi business card

Bowers designed this business card for make-up artist Pari Bijarzahi to promote herself to photographers, designers, and models. "It was important for Pari to have a way to approach these people, and sending her business cards and being able to give them out to contacts and clients is important," explains Bowers. "While doing this, she can also establish a brand for herself, so I developed her business identity to have a consistent format and logo to use on her letterhead, website, and so on." Bowers created Bijarzahi's logo using the P and B of her name and linking them together. The back of the card simply illustrates her profession. As Bowers explains, the card is the first point of contact for some people, and these illustrations make it clear she is a make-up artist. The cards are two-color print with metallic gold edges.

Client: **Remember a Day**
Design: **Simon Slater at LAKI 139**
Country: **UK**

Remember a Day postcard

LAKI 139 created this postcard to promote its sister company, Remember A Day, a bespoke wedding stationery service. The postcard shows past projects to give the customer an idea of the service LAKI 139 has to offer. LAKI 139 wanted an Art Deco/Art Nouveau feel, but with a modern twist. The font and border were drawn in Illustrator. Cards were printed on 400g matte stock which was matte laminated for extra durability.

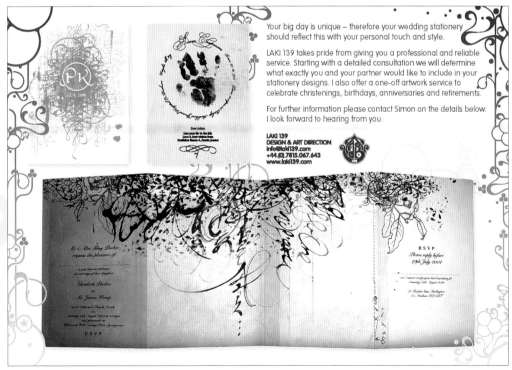

Client: **Jan Oksbøl Callesen/Mikael Forth**
Design: **Jan Oksbøl Callesen/Mikael Forth**
Country: **Denmark**

The Flaming Electricity Cat Child action playing cards

This card deck is part of the merchandise package for the computer game The Flaming Electricity Cat Child, created by Callesen and Forth. The game was never realized, but all its characters, themes, and merchandise were presented at the Copenhagen gallery RACA as part of a wider show. The cards shown here display some of the game's characters: hearts, the heroes; diamonds, the victims; clubs, miscellaneous bad guys; and spades, the multinational company (industrial or commercial) supervillains. As it is supposedly a computer game, the characters have all been composed of hand-drawn pixels. The typeface used is The Flaming Electricity Cat Child. The deck of cards was sold at the gallery RACA and through the game's website.

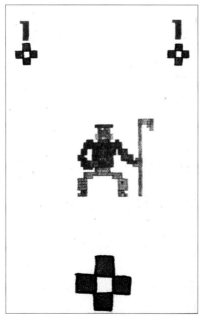

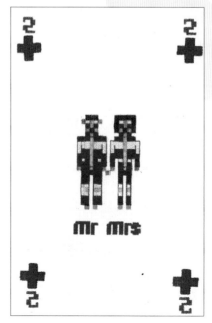

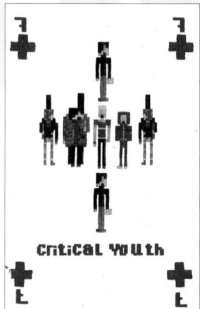

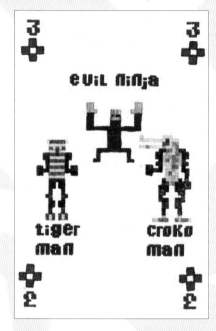

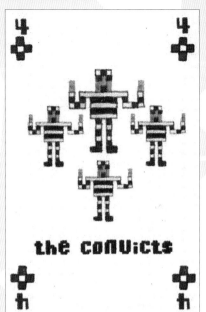

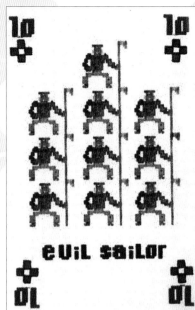

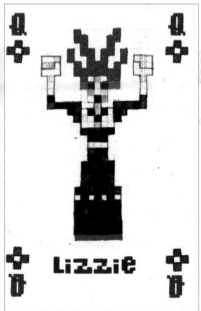

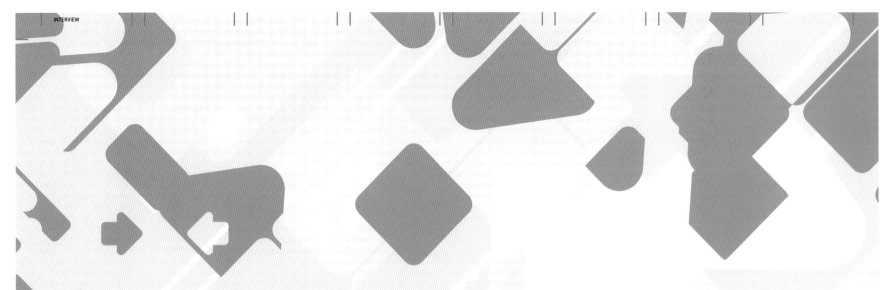

Kate Bingaman-Burt, Public Design Center/Obsessive Consumption, USA

How would you describe your working self?
I am a "by any means necessary" type of worker. I like to use whatever medium to get the job done most effectively. I do lots of illustration work, but also employ lots of hand assembly and printing as well as different media in my work.

What is most important when creating a business card or other promotional items for a company?
Creating something special—something that communicates effectively—but also making sure that you create a piece that the receiver wants to keep. Not only because the information that it contains is important, but also because they have just received a unique object and they want to hold on to it.

What makes one design successful over another?
If the piece is not only aesthetically pleasing, but also conceptually sound. I love the work of Futurefarmers. tremendously beautiful, yet they are also working with tight concepts and for a good cause. Nick Felton falls into this category as well. He takes something that could be very sterile (infographics) and fuses it with personal details and documentation.

How did you get into design?
I thought I wanted to be a journalist until someone told me that they liked my hand lettering and hired me to do a packaging project when I was 20. My English major was finished so I thought I would pick up a graphic design major as well. I realized one class, halfway into my graphic design course, that this was the field for me. It was like journalism in that I was communicating and able to investigate a variety of topics, but I liked having various tools at my disposal to achieve that, rather than just Microsoft Word.

What inspires your work?
Personal consumption, pop culture, found typography, vintage patterns, ephemera, sarcasm, irony, DIY culture, and new-wave craft culture.

What has been your favorite project to work on?
All of the work that I do for Obsessive Consumption is a favorite of mine because it is self-inflicted. Obsessive Consumption started when I decided to photograph all of my purchases and, in turn, create a brand out of the process that I could package and promote. I am currently hand-drawing all of my credit-card statements until they are paid off. I am also drawing something that I purchase each day along with making piles of work (zines, pillows, photographs, dresses, buttons, more drawings) that all fit into this brand, which simply mocks my own relationship with my purchases. Under the umbrella of Obsessive Consumption, I zoom back and forth between illustration, web design, product design, installation, sewing, and printmaking.

What would be your dream project to work on?
Between Obsessive Consumption and Public Design Center, I am able to work on a lot of amazing projects. My favorite projects are those that involve lots of drawing, color, and pieces and parts. I like making handmade multiples.

Clara Courtaigne, France/UK

How would you describe your working self?
I would describe myself as a craft-based designer.

You have designed some great interactive greetings cards...
Yes, all the greetings cards I designed actively involve both the sender and recipient of the card. The "I send you buttons because flowers die" and "Flat flowers" cards are based on the same concept: how to send flowers that last forever. The first set of cards I designed is the "I send you buttons because flowers die." This was an attempt to circumvent things that perish. It refers to a song by Jacques Brel entitled "I brought you sweets because flowers fade." The idea of using buttons came when I found amazing antique buttons at a flea market in Paris, which looked like flowers to me. The postcards shift perspectives on two levels by substituting buttons for flowers and a photo for the real object. The "flat flowers" cards were another fun and poetic way for me to send everlasting flowers. This time I tried to design a card that could be considered as an object instead of being just an image.

And what about the ones that involve recipient participation?
The "Dotty for you" and "A thousand words" projects were designed together with Richard Monk. We wanted to create a series of greetings cards that allowed the sender or recipient to have fun interacting with the card. The main idea behind both these sets is that make-your-own cards are more personal, and therefore more unique, and also more fun.

Why the interaction?
I cannot imagine my work without interaction. I think all images are designed for a specific person or people, and part of the pleasure of design is eliciting reactions from people.

What do you think is the most important thing about creating a greetings card?
The most important thing to me is to capture the imagination of the recipient so that she or he will keep the card.

What makes one design successful over another?
I believe that what makes a card stand out is not only the quality of the image, but also the message that image conveys.

How did you get into design?
I guess I started design thanks to a beautiful box of oil pastels we had at home when I was a child. And I got into it more deeply through a Graphic Design degree in London.

What has been your favorite project to work on?
The next one!

03

"We have a collection of letterpress type and a small press in the studio, which is always good to play on and use when appropriate."

Chris Turnbull, UK

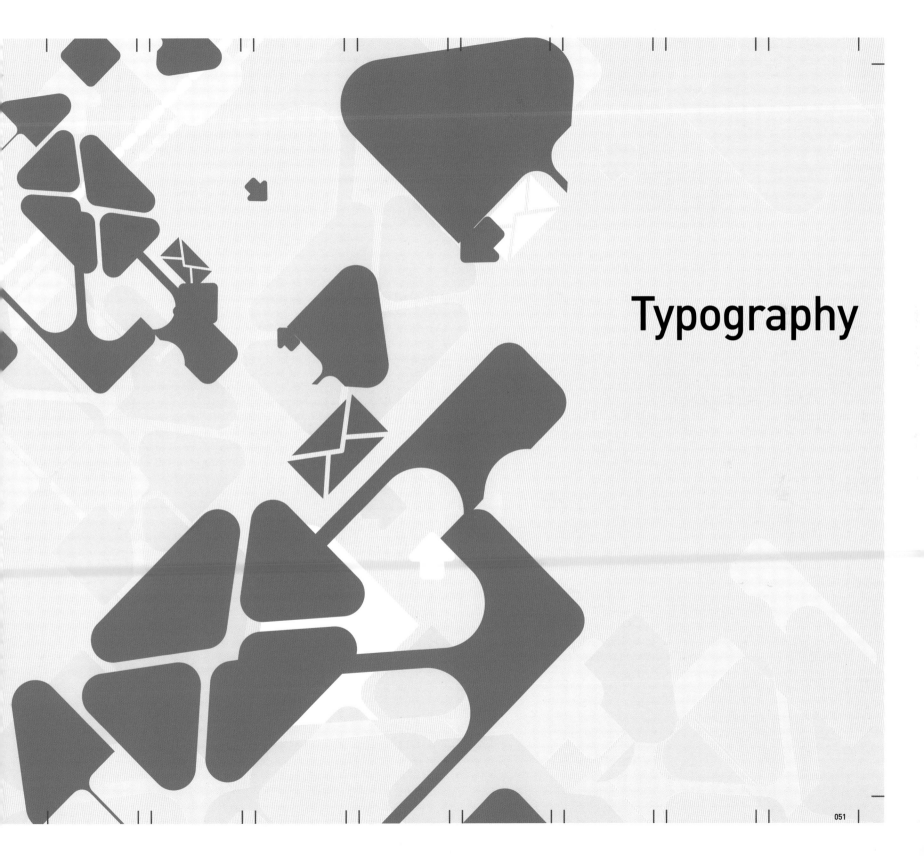

Typography

Introduction

Typography is present in design not only to inform us of something, or communicate information, but also to give the design piece a "voice." It is important that the choice of typeface and typographic layout works together to convey information clearly. It must also be relevant to and fit with the company or person it is conveying the information on behalf of. There is much interesting, experimental, and bold use of typography within the design of the cards in this chapter. The examples throughout this chapter show how designers use typography both to communicate and to illustrate, and how a simple business card can be transformed into a design classic through the clever choice of type and the innovative use of typographic layout.

"I believe that what makes a card stand out is not only the quality of the image, but also the message that image conveys."

Clara Courtaigne, France/UK

Client: **NODE Berlin Oslo**
Design: **Anders Hofgaard**
　　at **NODE Berlin Oslo**
Country: **Germany**

NODE Berlin Oslo
business cards

NODE Berlin Oslo created these business cards using letterpress to overprint its studio contact details on old Estonian business cards. "The inspiration came from seeing this old letterpress facility in Tallinn, Estonia, that was still being used for printing business cards," explains Hofgaard. "They had stacks of old cards lying around, ranging from escort services to the Estonian police, and the letterpress technique allowed us to overprint on them." The result is a series of cards on which the added information always remains the same, but the background changes. "The cards show all kinds of graphic design (good and bad), and this shows how content is influenced by its graphic environment," adds Hofgaard. Russian letterpress Grotesque typeface was chosen as it did not interfere with the existing designs.

Client: **Little Yellow Jacket**
Design: **Zoë Bather at Studio8 Design**
Country: **UK**

Little Yellow Jacket mailer

Studio8 Design created this mailer for Little Yellow Jacket, a bespoke digital hire company. "Little Yellow Jacket wanted a beautiful piece that would communicate that they were the best in the market, and that was also very practical and flexible in its use," explains Bather. "Digital hire can sound quite technical and complicated so they wanted to break it down into simple chunks." With the postcard book format, each one of Little Yellow Jacket's services has its own card.

To strike the balance between a book and a set of cards, Studio8 Design created the mailer so that the large words (which appear on each card and wrap around onto the reverse) read as a list of services when flicking through the book. However, if the cards are torn out, the words make sense as titles to the cards. American Typewriter typeface has been used with Opti Gaucho for the large words. The company logo has been blocked in gloss black foil onto front and back covers.

Client: **University of the Arts London**
Design: **Chris Turnbull at Turnbull Grey**
Country: **UK**

Governors' Dinner invitation

The Chairman of the University of the Arts, London, hosts the annual Governors' Dinner. "We have worked with UAL for a number of years and have a good idea of what they like and don't like," explains Turnbull. "The idea with this invite was to create a tactile, engaging object that had high production values and looked exclusive. As an arts-based organization the UAL appreciates the 'craft' element of design, and on this occasion we wanted to use letterpress in a different way by foil-blocking it in matte silver foil." Turnbull Grey added texture by using an embossed stock and duplexing it to another colored stock. "We wanted something simple and bold on the front and tried various different words, but in the end the word Dinner worked best and had the right sense of occasion," he adds. "We set the text from our letterpress collection, proofed, and scanned it to make the artwork." The text on the reverse is set in FS Lola.

Client: **TNOP™ Design**
Design: **Tnop Wangsillapakun at TNOP™ Design**
Country: **USA**

Have a Nice Day postcard

Wangsillapakun created these postcards as part of an experimental typographic art project. "The idea behind this piece was to experiment with typography and its silhouettes as art... I have a total of three or more ideas in this series, but this is the first one in the set. The blue pattern is intended to draw the viewer's attention away from the typography shape," adds Wangsillapakun. "Then when you touch the artwork, you'll feel the texture of the paper and letterpress printing technique." The typeface used is a custom font based on Arial Black and the card has been letterpressed on a beermat stock.

Client: **Stefan Boublil/The Apartment**
Design: **Peter Crnokrak at ±**
Country: **USA**

The Apartment business cards

Crnokrak illustrated/designed these cards for creative design agency The Apartment as part of its new identity package and website. The primary design brief was to create a conversation piece that personified the ethos of the studio—romantic minimalism. As such, all print pieces (except envelopes) come packaged in bound pads of thin sheets of paper, reminiscent of classic writing tablets. The business cards feature an abbreviated list of tag categories derived from the studio's cultural design portal. Each business card tablet is a stack of 12 different cards (with different combinations of website tags) repeated eight times (96 cards per tablet). Tablets of 96 cards were bound together using standard edge-on glue binding techniques.

Client: **Philippe Archontakis**
Design: **Philippe Archontakis**
Country: **Canada**

Philippe Archontakis business card

"Business cards are a quick way to show the client your quality work, and your professionalism in the field," Archontakis explains. "I wanted to promote as much as possible my website and my portfolio, so, my logo is my URL, big and bold. I've wanted something simple, timeless, and with a 'chic' factor. So black on black was the answer." A modified Helvetica Neue typeface together with Akkurat was used for the card, which was created using a black foil stamp on a black stock.

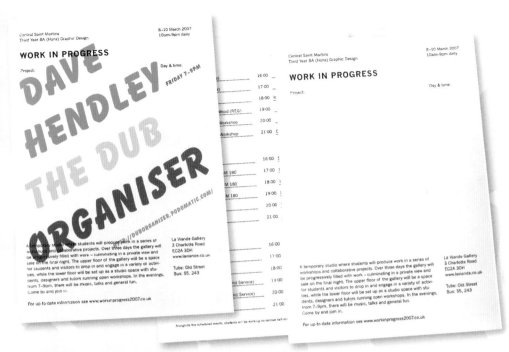

Client: **Emmi**
Design: **Emmi Salonen at Emmi**
Country: **UK**

Emmi Season's Greetings badge card

Emmi Salonen designed this promotional, seasonal greeting to send to friends, clients, and suppliers. "I wanted to have a seasonal card that didn't necessarily celebrate 'Christmas,' but instead the season's spirit," explains Salonen. "I also wanted to do a limited-edition card that was fun and worked as a gift, not purely as a throwaway card, so the card includes two badges: a red badge that says 'NO' on the side and a green one saying 'YES.' The idea was that by wearing one you can either make a statement about the season or just wear it as an accessory."

Client: **Work in Progress**
Design: **Oscar Bauer/Matt Bucknall/
Jennie Hancock/Ewan Robertson**
Country: **UK**

Work in Progress flier

Work in Progress is an exhibition in the form of an open studio trying to capture the essence of "work in progress" by creating a social, interactive, ephemeral situation. Alongside student-initiated work, guest designers and course tutors were invited to run short workshops. All work featured in the exhibition was created within three days and the private view was held on the last night. Bauer, Bucknall, Hancock, and Robertson created a flier template for each person in the exhibition to promote their own projects or workshops. "We printed all the fliers and put stacks out so that people either could make one-offs or do overprinting/photocopying," explains Bauer. "The first run, which we laser-printed on recycled card from Paperback, showed an empty schedule and one sponsor, Paperback. The second run had the timetable part filled in and the name of another sponsor, Cobra beer. The third had an almost full schedule. It was interesting to have the flier for a work-in-progress show as a work in progress."

Client: **London College of Communication**
Design: **Mark El-khatib/Claire McManus/
Henrik Tandberg**
Screen Printing: **Magnus Polbratt/
Ben Prescott/Samanta Vega**
Country: **UK**

TYPE-OH! invitation

El-khatib, McManus, and Tandberg
designed these invites for the 2007 BA
Typo/Graphic Design graduate degree
show. "The invites had to promote us
as a graduating collective in an exciting
and engaging way to some of the hardest
critics: the graphic design industry,"
explains El-khatib. "The aim of the
degree show was to subvert people's
expectations of what typo/graphic design
work could be. The show featured very
diverse and forward-thinking work, and
this was something we wanted to reflect
in its identity. Its name 'TYPE-OH!' was a
starting point in setting the tone of voice."
Each invite has only one quarter of the
image screenprinted on the reverse,
providing an intriguing teaser for the
show where the whole image can be
seen. With the typography on the front,
the design injected some personality
and rhythm into the type, by using a
contrast of scale and by setting the
type at an angle. The main image is a
photograph of several members of the
class physically spelling out the show's
name (Magnus Polbratt, T; Lisa Holst, Y;
Mark El-khatib, P; Samanta Vega, E;
Henrik Tandberg, O; James Melaugh, H;
Claire McManus, !). Gravur Condensed
typeface was used on the invitation.

As Text

"My dream job is anything atonal black and white, only type, set in one font, and printed on bond paper."

Peter Crnokrak, UK

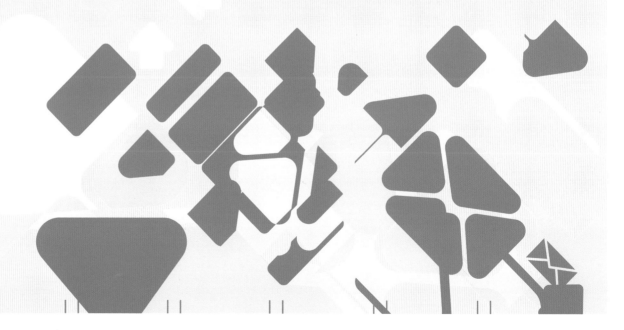

Client: **Tanya Leighton/CCA Glasgow**
Design: **Katrin Tüffers/Markus Weisbeck at Surface**
Countries: **Germany/UK**

In the Poem About Love You Don't Write the Word Love invitation

Leighton commissioned Surface to create this invite for a group show she curated at the Centre for Contemporary Arts in Glasgow, Scotland. "After receiving the exhibition title, we worked on this idea, designing from the typographical direction something in a nineteenth-century poem style with a strong link to '60s concrete poetry," explains Tüffers. The result is a simple typographic-based invitation printed on an uncoated Munken colored stock. The typeface is Futura ND.

mm^TM

Matthias Mächler | textmaechler

Forchstrasse 72, CH-8008 Zürich
+41 43 488 63 00, Mobile +41 79 667 89 27
matthias@textmaechler.ch
Texte nach Mass: www.textmaechler.ch

mm^TM
weiter im Text...

Matthias Mächler | textmaechler

Forchstrasse 72, CH-8008 Zürich
+41 43 488 63 00, Mobile +41 79 667 89 27
matthias@textmaechler.ch
Texte nach Mass: **www.textmaechler.ch**

Client: **Matthias Mächler**
Design: **Friedrich-Wilhelm Graf**
  at unfolded
Country: **Switzerland**

Matthias Mächler | Textmaechler business card

unfolded created this business card for Matthias Mächler as part of his identity, with the brief to include his name, address, and URL. "We've developed the logo setting, stationery (ranging from lettersheets, stickers, stamps to postcards), and a small, simple website," explains Graf.

"We combined his initials 'mm' with his title 'textmaechler' (old Swiss-German for 'textmaker') to create a logo for him." The thin blue lines (usually used on index cards and ruled paper) are a reference to his work as a writer. Interstate typeface has been used for the main text, and the logo was developed from it.

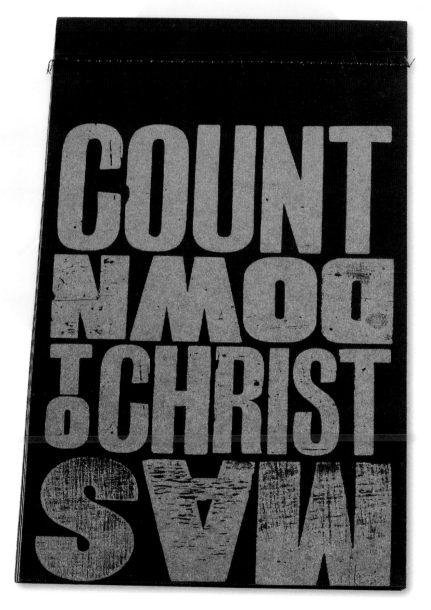

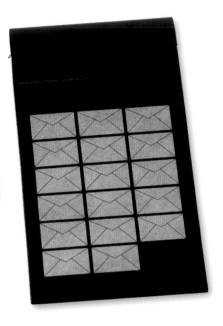

Client: **Turnbull Grey**
Design: **Chris Turnbull at Turnbull Grey**
Country: **UK**

Countdown to Christmas
card/Advent calendar

Turnbull Grey designed this Christmas card/Advent calendar mailer as an alternative to a regular Christmas card. "We wanted to create something that would be noticed and interacted with," explains Turnbull. "We wanted to draw on the universal experience of Christmas in a humorous way; we chatted about what Christmas meant to us in the studio and researched Christmas facts around the numbers 24 to 1, then illustrated them typographically. The pages of the Countdown are torn off day by day until you reach One." The card/calendar was printed in silver ink on an ebony color stock before being Singer-sewn, with perforations created to enable the pages to be torn off.

Client: **Plug**
Design: **Peter and Paul**
Country: **UK**

Plug business cards

Peter and Paul created this business card for the directors and staff of Plug as part of the club's new brand identity. "They wanted the cards to be different and stand out while pushing the new identity strongly," explains Paul Reardon. "There were around eight different names which we needed to consider." The card design is a direct enlargement of the logo and the same size as an actual British electrical plug. Monospace 821 Bold typeface has been used throughout the identity for its utilitarian and technical feel and has been blind-embossed on the business card. All individual personal details were then printed onto red stickers that were designed to mimic the rating stickers on plugs. The cards can then be used generically or personalized.

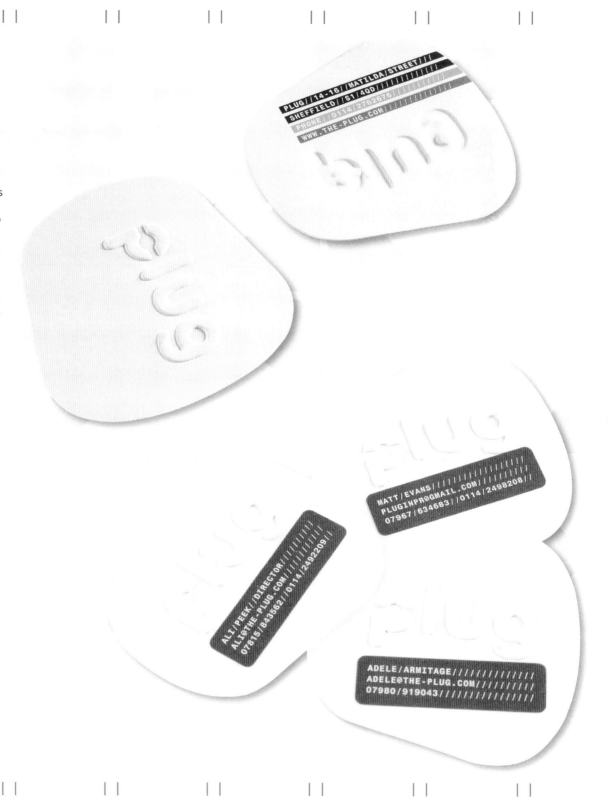

BROWN INK ON PINK DUPLEXED COLORPLAN 540GSM BAGDAD BROWN & CANDY PINK

Design by Parent
Print by Generation Press

PINK INK ON BROWN DUPLEXED COLORPLAN 540GSM BAGDAD BROWN & CANDY PINK

Design by Parent
Print by Generation Press

Client: **Generation Press**
Design: **Chris Harman at Parent**
Country: **UK**

Generation Press promotional cards

"We were working on a similar idea for a client and Generation asked us to design a card for them to promote the printing technique to their clients," explains Harman. "We wanted to show off a funky edge to the company using a technique that was unfamiliar, and decided to explain the technique that we used to create the card within the design itself."

Parent has used laminated sheets of two different-color Colorplan boards with a screen print in the opposing color on each side. It is a simple, effective execution, and the laminated board provides an interesting level of detail not always noticed on first inspection. Aachen and Plantin typefaces have been used throughout.

Client: **Pierre Vanni**
Design: **Pierre Vanni**
Country: **France**

I AM business card

Vanni wanted to create a business card for himself that was fresh and serious, with all the necessary contact details. "I love Japanese imagery so I wanted to incorporate this into the design, but in a very subtle way," explains Vanni. "Also I wanted to create a card that had contrast and humility between older, more serious graphics and younger, fresher ideas." The card also had to reflect Vanni's work with paper and paper craft. He created his I AM logo by hand by repeating the letter P over and over in rows.

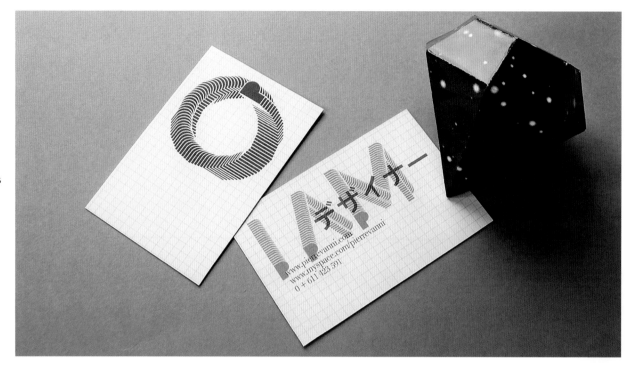

Client: **Central Saint Martins College of Art & Design**
Design: **Oscar Bauer**
Country: **UK**

In Celebration of Alan Fletcher invitation

Bauer created this invite for a celebratory talk about the late Alan Fletcher. "'So, what does one design for a design legend like Alan Fletcher?' was my starting point," explains Bauer, "and also what made me not design at all." Bauer set the necessary type simply on the invite front and then wrote "Write or draw something for Alan and bring to the celebration" on the back. The invitation was sent out with a pencil so guests and friends of Alan could make something on the back and bring it to the talk. "When the talk happened, I pinned all the invites on the wall so that people could have a look, and then all the invites went to Alan's family," explains Bauer. The guests kept the pencils that read "In Celebration of Alan Fletcher" in foil block.

Client: **Lucie Matějčková/Petr Dvořáček**
Design: **Filip Heyduk at Heyduk,**
   Musil & Strnad
Country: **Czech Republic**

Lucie & Petr
wedding invitation

Heyduk designed this wedding invitation
for his two friends, Lucie Matějčková
and Petr Dvořáček. The invitation has
been divided into three different cards
to announce the wedding ceremony,
family lunch, and party for friends, with
the idea to send to each guest whichever
of the cards were appropriate. Each
of the typography-based cards features
a self-adhesive note, highlighting the
date and time of each particular event
with a map of the venue on the reverse.
The notes could be removed from the
card and stuck on the recipient's fridge
or computer, or in their diaries. Wafle,
a new, modern, clean typeface, has been
used throughout.

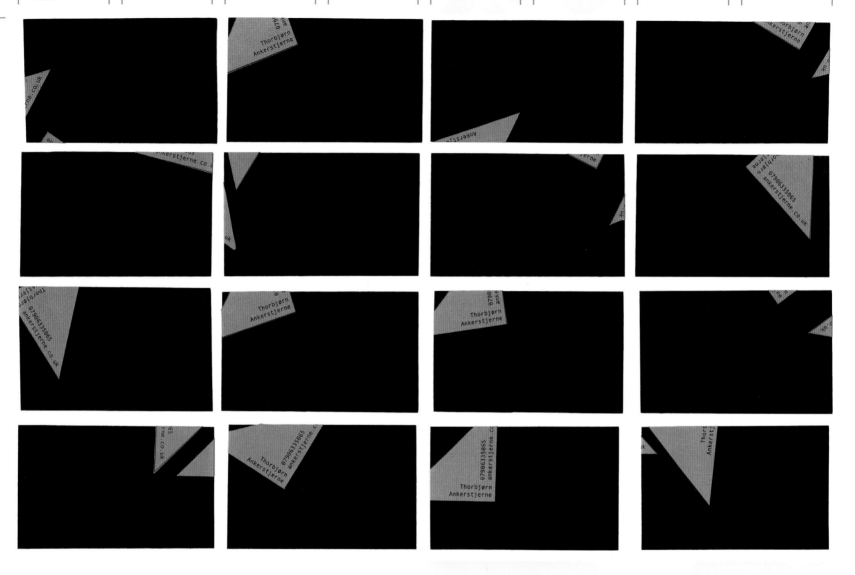

Client: **Thorbjørn Ankerstjerne**
Design: **Thorbjørn Ankerstjerne**
Country: **UK**

Thorbjørn Ankerstjerne business cards

Ankerstjerne designed this card for himself following his graduation from Central Saint Martins College, London. "I wanted something to hand over that was a unique item," explains Ankerstjerne, "so that each person I gave it to knew that what they received was just for them, very personal. People see that my business cards are all different, and quite often they ask to pick one for themselves." The only imagery on the business card is the fluorescent triangle. "For me the triangle is very visually arresting; it also has the ability to be wrapped around both sides of the card and create interesting shapes," adds Ankerstjerne. He has used Andale Mono typeface, a monospaced sans serif that accommodates the business card's general design simplicity.

Client: **Brandoctor**
Art Direction: **Siniša Sudar**
Design: **Maja Benčić at Brandoctor**
Country: **Croatia**

Brandoctor Pills business cards

"Our business cards were made to resemble a box of medicine with all the essential information of a regular business card printed on it in a fun and creative way," explains Maja Benčić. "The names of our employees have each been changed to resemble a 'medicine-like' name, and every 'medicine' has its own purpose. For example, the surname 'Minkara' became 'Minkaren Forte' and includes pills that help boost creativity (Minkara being the Creative Director); the surname 'Manasteriotti' changed to 'Manastelizin,' which contains ten pills for improvement of visual identity (art director); and 'Bauer' changed to 'Bauersdorf' for brand boosting (senior brand consultant)." The real names were then printed in smaller text with bar-code numbers for cell-phone numbers and "solution" numbers for dates of birth to complete this well-designed package. Finally the box contains mints in blister packs. Sudar designed Brandoctor's logo and Franklin Gothic has been used for all Brandoctor corporate materials.

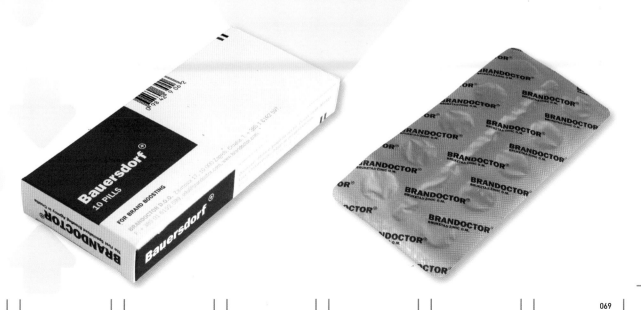

Client: **Krisztian Zana**
Design: **Serge Seidlitz**
Country: **UK**

Krisztian Zana business card

Zana wanted a simple business card with his name, occupation, and contact details, all rendered with hand-drawn typography. "This logo emphasizes Krisztian's name and is bold in style and color," explains Seidlitz. "I drew the letters by hand, scanned them, and colored them on my Mac." The reverse of the card has been kept plain and set in a bright, bold red.

Client: **Wigan Little Theatre**
Design: **MARK Studio**
Country: **UK**

Little Theatre card

MARK Studio designed this business card for one of the UK's best and oldest amateur theaters, Wigan Little Theatre. Inspired by the theater's name, it produced an appropriately sized business card (and subsequent stationery) for the theater—all slightly smaller than the usual dimensions. "When people receive one, it always raises a smile" explains Mark Lester. It is a simple, yet effective business card.

Client: **Ben Weeks**
Design: **Ben Weeks**
Country: **Canada**

Ben Weeks business card/ bookmark

"I'd sent another project off to the printer (Somerset Graphics) and it turned out there was a bit of extra space on the printing plate, so I made the card and bookmark in about 10 minutes and sent them to the printer by FTP," explains Weeks. "My cards were always handmade before, quite a time-consuming affair, so this was an opportunity to make something consistent with the look of my website." His cards could help him to build relationships and his reputation. "Having someone visit my website and e-mail me seemed a good way to do that," he adds. "On top of that there is my name and what I do—everything else is secondary." Avant Garde and Lubalin Graph typefaces have been used throughout. "They work nicely together because they have similar shapes and were designed by the same man," explains Weeks. "I'd seen the combination used before to good effect." The letters are debossed, giving the effect of letterpress and a subtle tactile quality that helps to differentiate the cards from most standard business cards.

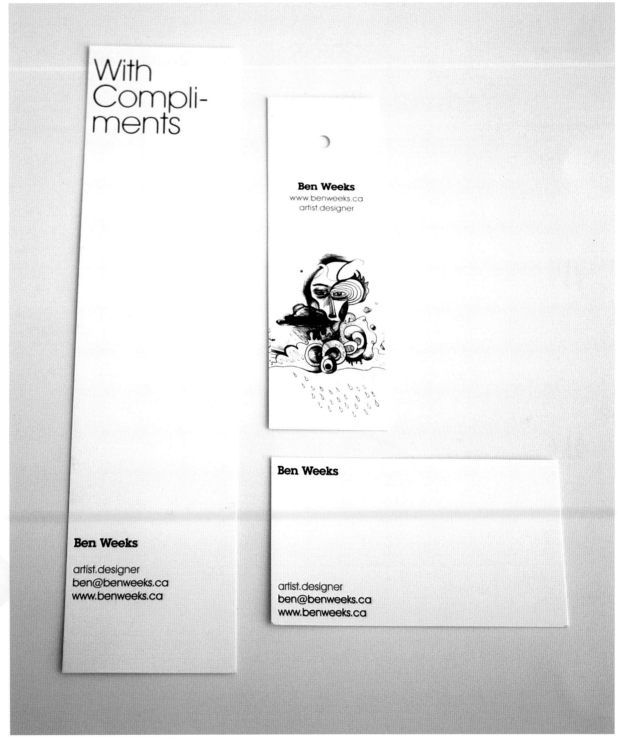

Client: **Peter and Paul**
Design: **Peter and Paul**
Country: **UK**

Peter and Paul
business cards

Peter and Paul designed this innovative
and memorable business card as part of
their wider stationery set. "We designed
all our stationery to have a Peter side and
a Paul side, which made total sense as
that's our company name," explains Paul
Reardon. "We'd also used laser-cutting
and etching a fair bit in other projects and
felt it a really elegant tool, which is why
we decided to create the stenciled logo."
The logo, set in Roadworks typeface,
is laser-cut and the text is laser-etched
on an embossed black Colorplan stock.

Client: **Mississippi State University College of Architecture, Art, and Design**
Design: **Clifton Burt/Kate Bingaman-Burt**
Country: **USA**

Gulf Coast Community Design handout

"In the aftermath of Hurricane Katrina, it became clear to area architects and related designers that the establishment of a community design studio would be a critical piece of the rebuilding efforts," explains Bingaman-Burt. "This piece was somewhat exploratory as we searched for a visual 'voice' for the Katrina recovery.

As Mississippi designers, our Community Design Centers were actively involved in the rebuilding efforts." The designers used the color orange to apply all text and imagery to the card because of its strong association with construction. The card was screenprinted using a Gocco printer.

analog

Magazin für Netzlese und Blogkultur

Christburger Straße 3

10405 Berlin

beta:www.analog-magazin.de

==================================

Svenja von Döhlen

svenja@analog-magazin.de

+49.176.240 320 53

Client: **ANALOG Magazine**
Design: **Svenja von Döhlen at Formdusche**
Country: **Germany**

ANALOG Magazine
business card

ANALOG covers news on Internet selection and blog culture. This card was designed with a subtle nod to the magazine concept. von Döhlen applied the magazine's bookmarks—orange sticker dots—which readers can use to mark their favorites as they read the magazine, like digital bookmarks in a web browser, to the card. These are added by hand, giving a hand-made feel as each card is a little different. Makimango and Mono typefaces, the magazine's fonts, are used throughout.

Client: **Alex Marshall**
Design: **Emmi Salonen at Emmi**
Country: **UK**

Alex Marshall business card

Salonen designed this card for freelance journalist Alex Marshall. His brief was for something unique to reflect what he does, with a small, special detail within the finishing—he wanted something simple, but clever. "The idea is based on us folding corners of magazines on the pages that we find interesting and want to remember," explains Salonen. "The idea was taken as it is, and by folding a corner of the business card the same reaction is created. People can relate to this small action and the card has been a success in terms of people remembering my client and even once commissioning him purely on the basis of the card." The back of the card has a pattern that creates a contrast when the corner is folded to the white "info" side. Storno typeface has been used for its typewriter feel.

Client: **Erin Skrypek**
Design: **Roanne Adams**
Country: **USA**

Erin Skrypek business card

Erin Skrypek, a freelance fashion and beauty editorial writer, commissioned Adams to create a business card that represented her style. "Erin is a hot chick, she flies around town interviewing interesting people and attending parties," explains Adams, "so I thought that a bird would be the perfect mascot for her on her business card." Adams drew the bird herself and chose to use FIG, a beautiful, modern monoline script, to "reflect her ladylike, yet hard-working manner." The card was printed on simple perforated printer paper. Adams supplied Skrypek with a Word template so that she could print her own cards.

Client: **BURO-GDS**
Design: **Ellen Zhao at BURO-GDS**
Country: **USA**

BURO-GDS business card

Zhao designed this business card, which features English and French. "My own work is very much about reaching out, trying to jump over the invisible, but profound space/gap between two people," she explains. "It is also about highlighting and transforming a mundane experience into a moment. In this case, the normal practice of passing a business card is changed into something more personal, sometimes whimsical, and nonsensical. The French part uses the informal form of 'you' (*tu* instead of *vous*), creating a more unusual experience." Once the card is filled out, the interaction between the handwritten and printed text creates an image of a little note with a phone number that someone leaves. The idea is that it can be serious, but also flirtatious.

dear ~~cher~~ chère
Mariam
i love j'adore
your sense of humor
i'd like to je voudrais bien
meet you at the park
please write to me at écris-moi à **ellen.zhao@web.de**
call me at appelle-moi au
+33 (0)6 72 20 32 89 or ou **+1 718 478 3364**
see the site regarde le site **buro-gds.com**

dear cher ~~chère~~
Jean-Pierre
i love j'adore
your drawings
i'd like to je voudrais bien
visite your studio
please write to me at écris-moi à **ellen.zhao@web.de**
call me at appelle-moi au
+33 (0)6 72 20 32 89 or ou **+1 718 478 3364**
see the site regarde le site **buro-gds.com**

dear cher ~~chère~~
antoine
i love j'adore
tes chaussures
i'd like to je voudrais bien
voir R.B. avec toi
please write to me at écris-moi à **ellen.zhao@web.de**
call me at appelle-moi au
+33 (0)6 72 20 32 89 or ou **+1 718 478 3364**
see the site regarde le site **buro-gds.com**

dear ~~cher~~ chère
Pauline
i love j'adore
les lapins roses
i'd like to je voudrais bien
manger des tajines avec toi
please write to me at écris-moi à **ellen.zhao@web.de**
call me at appelle-moi au
+33 (0)6 72 20 32 89 or ou **+1 718 478 3364**
see the site regarde le site **buro-gds.com**

dear cher chère

i love j'adore

i'd like to je voudrais bien

please write to me at écris-moi à **ellen.zhao@web.de**
call me at appelle-moi au
+33 (0)6 72 20 32 89 or ou **+1 718 478 3364**
see the site regarde le site **buro-gds.com**

Client: **Mississippi State University Graphic Design Department**
Design: **Kate Bingaman-Burt/Public Design Center**
Country: **USA**

Crap Detector website promotional packs

When Bingaman-Burt, Assistant Professor of Graphic Design at Mississippi State University, decided to start a website for all of her classes, she also wanted to give her students fun packs to celebrate the launch. "I designed the stickers and buttons to advertise crapdetector.com not only so that the students wouldn't forget the site address, but so that they would get excited about it as well," she explains. "It needed to be cheap and awesome. I wanted to make a sticker of the logo and the address so they would stick it on their notebook or binder. My students love buttons as well, so I created logo buttons to go along with the stickers." The logotype is set in Bookman Swash Italic and the little computer with the heart is a modified stock image. She had 100 packs made and handed them out to her students on the first day of class.

Client: **DRY Soda Company**
Design: **Steve Watson at Turnstyle**
Country: **USA**

DRY Soda business card

Turnstyle created the DRY Soda Company packaging and brand identity, including its business card as shown here. "The aim of DRY Soda is to attract a discerning culinary audience," explains Watson. "In a fashion similar to fine wines, the sodas were developed specifically to be paired with great foods. The client wanted the stationery we designed to echo the bottle design that we created: sophistication through minimalism without being cold and clinical." This entails boiling information down to its typographic essence. The custom-drawn company logo is based on Helvetica. The card has been letterpress-printed on eggshell-textured uncoated paper, lending warmth to the otherwise minimalist typography.

DRY.™ www.drysoda.com

SODA CO: BREEANNA MARCHITTO
T 206.652.2345 ext. 108 / F 206.652.8284
M 206.499.2905 / E breeanna@drysoda.com
410 First Avenue South / Seattle, WA 98104

Ariel Aguilera & Andrea Benyi, Pandarosa, Australia/Germany

How would you describe your working selves?
Contemporary visual artists.

Can you tell me about your work?
Most of the work included is invites for exhibition openings, which are always nice to do as you can treat them as a further piece of artwork within the show; in this way they became part of the show and not simply directional information tools. The rest is mainly business cards, which have to be more informational and practical.

What do you think is the most important thing about creating an invite?
Creating a sense of interactivity between the object (invite) and the receiver (audience).

What makes one design successful over another?
How you feel about it. I guess design is an emotive art form, you do it till it feels right. Having the correct opening dates, times, and contact details also helps.

How did you get into design?
Hard to say, maybe it started when we both drew on cigarette packets as children or after we completed our degrees at university. I don't think we got into design because of design, but due to numerous visual and nonvisual influences in our youth. I like to think that we are still learning, though.

What inspires your work?
There is no "general" or "singular" inspirational point, as that would be really ignorant of us. I think there are too many factors to take into consideration, but overall seeing people taking chances is always inspiring, as well as the only guaranteed certainty in life, which is change.

What would be your dream invite project to work on?
An interactive one. Something the receiver has to touch or complete somehow in order to get to the venue, etc. I think in a digital age it is important to maintain a connection to our analog self and create "actual" real interaction between people and the objects they receive.

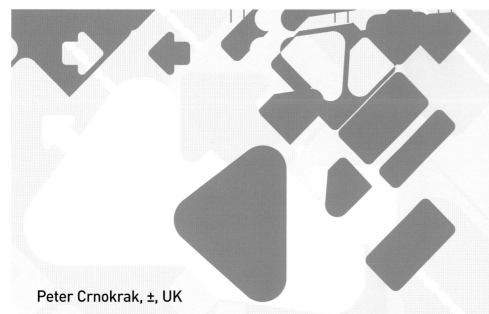

Peter Crnokrak, ±, UK

How would you describe your working self?
How I describe myself is dependent not on who I am *per se*, but rather what type of project I'm working on at the moment. This is a purposeful adaptability of approach that allows one to explore fully the myriad avenues of communication possible. I've created pieces that are pure illustrations for exhibitions, pieces that use only type for editorial layout, etc. It seems such adaptability is becoming more and more common among designers today. There is a new generation of designers that sees no boundary between commercial and self-initiated work—it is this self-redefinition that pushes the individual to explore and create new means by which to communicate.

Can you tell me about the work that is in this book?
The ± business card is an attempt to encapsulate my design ethos. Self-defining work (identity, cards, portfolio) is widely considered the most difficult to execute—where do you start and where do you end? The ± business card is both simple and complex—I like extreme dichotomies. The e-mail only information side recognizes what is truly essential—the e-mail address contains my website URL where you can find my name and information. The dot grid on the reverse shows my interest in information design—the hand-appliqué graphite dot personifies the unique in the common: everything is the same and, at the same time, totally unique.

What do you think is the most important thing about creating a business card, invite, or other promo items?
Some level of basic information is required. If it's not complete, then it needs to lead to where further information can be accessed. Outside of that, it should be a conceptual portrait of the person/company.

What makes one design successful over another?
Interest. All communication design needs to appeal to one aspect of human interest or another—be it visual or intellectual, or a combination of the two. Speaking from my own process, I try to impart a strong conceptual underpinning to all my work, but am keenly aware of how best to express that idea through a visual language that appeals to the senses.

What inspires your work?
Inspiration comes from interest—I have too many interests to list completely—information design, politics, sociology, etc. But maybe that is the best description of who I am—someone with too many interests.

What would be your dream project to work on?
I love limitation—the fewer choices to make, the more fluid the design process. My dream job is anything atonal black and white, only type, set in one font, and printed on bond paper.

04

"The most important thing in the design of an invitation is to create a sense of interactivity between the object (invite) and the receiver (audience)."

Ariel Aguilera and Andrea Benyi, Australia/Germany

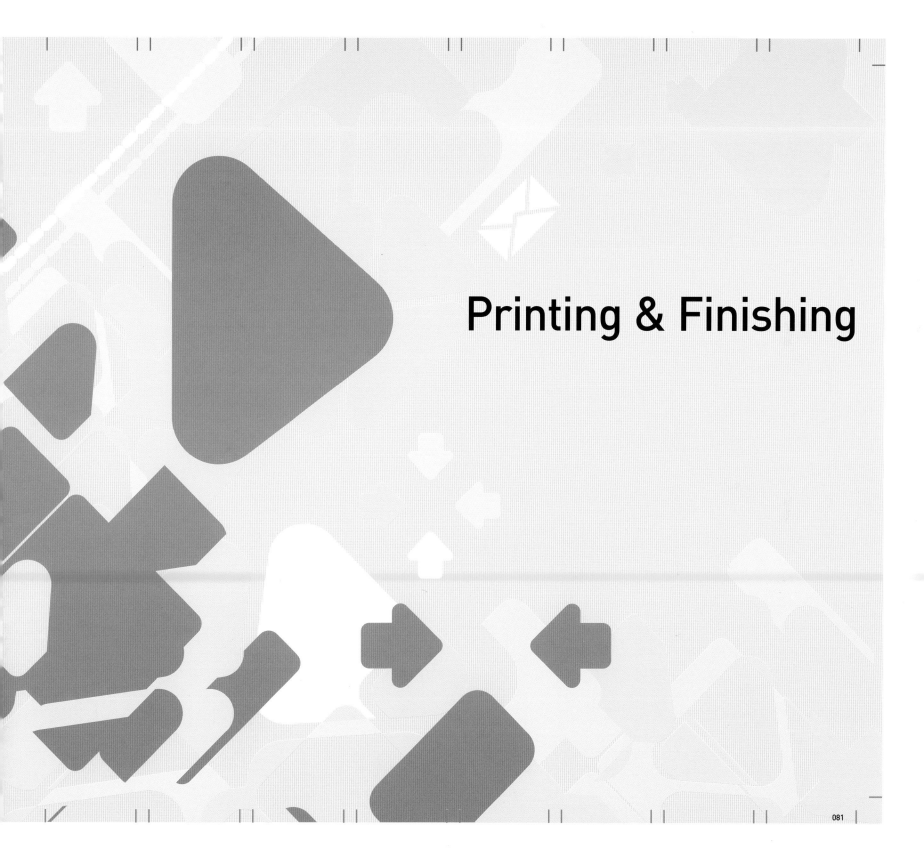

Printing & Finishing

Introduction

The printing techniques that can be used to differentiate one card from the rest are many and varied, and as this chapter shows, so are the materials that can be used to print them on. Even if the budget is limited there are simple, inexpensive ways to make a print design job stand out from the rest. From the choice of paper stock, inks, and printing finishes, each is as important as the artwork or typography on a particular card, and ultimately adds great character and individuality to the overall design. Examples on the following pages include the use, not only of unusual paper and card stocks, but also of materials such as plastic, and in one case vinyl. And, of course, there are many great examples of the use of paper-manipulation techniques such as embossing and die-cutting, which are far from uncommon techniques these days, but still fulfill the valuable role of setting a piece of design apart.

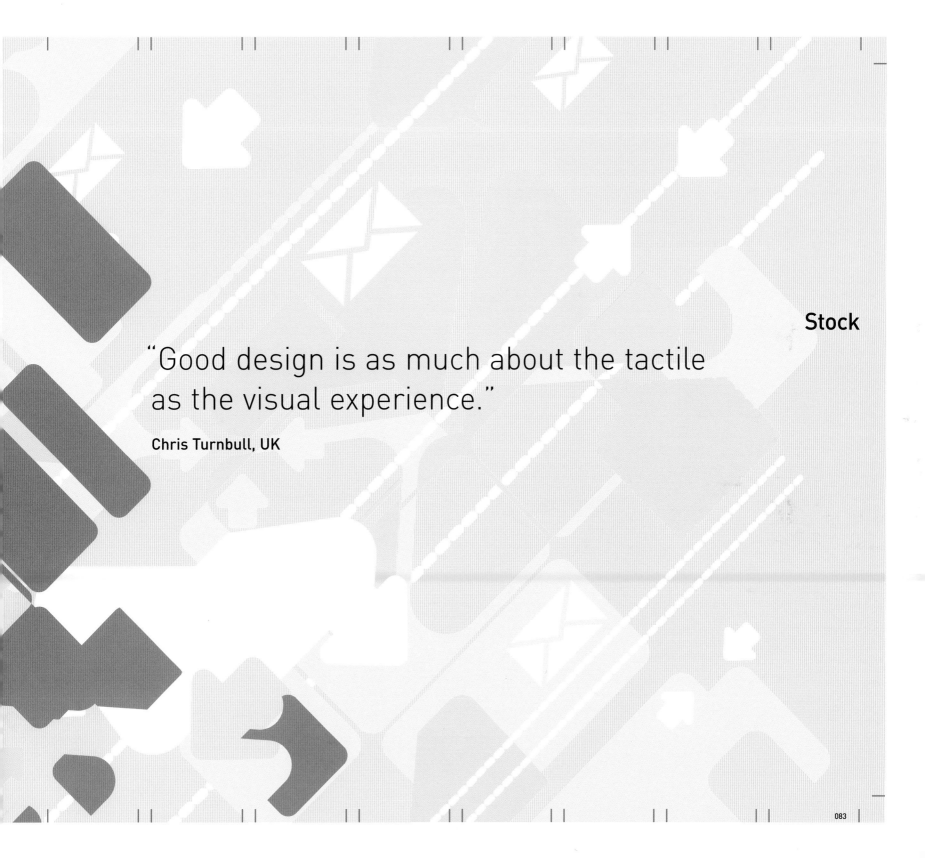

Stock

"Good design is as much about the tactile as the visual experience."

Chris Turnbull, UK

Client: **Muotohiomo Oy Ltd.**
Design: **Noa Bembibre**
Country: **Finland**

Muotohiomo Christmas card

This card was created for Muotohiomo, a small, but growing design studio in Helsinki, and Fine, a design-importing firm that operates within Muotohiomo. As designer Bembibre explains, "The main requirement of the card was that it would be cheap, but still effective—it had to be noticeable within the avalanche of cards and greetings received every Christmas... I wanted it to be really simple, no flashy effects, no shocking graphics, just very calm and subtle." The result is a card in which Bembibre has concentrated mainly on the copy to create the graphics. The typeface used is Berthold Akzidenz Grotesk Light. The text has been printed on very fine tracing paper in one color, pink, which is also Muotohiomo's color de facto. The card was printed on one side only and when folded, the print is still visible. The feel is fragile and quiet, which is in keeping with the copy.

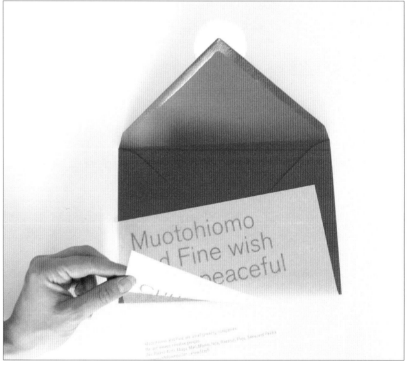

Client: **London College of Communication**
Design: **Sofia Leverbeck at Studio-SM**
Country: **UK**

Watching the Beaver Building its Dam Gave me an Idea invitation

Leverbeck designed this invite for a one-night exhibition featuring 15 designers including herself. Based on the theme of "breaking the boundaries between the art and the audience," everything in the exhibition could be taken away so that at the end of the night the space was empty.

The invite idea linked with this theme. With the restriction of a tight budget, the printing method had to be considered carefully. "The invite was printed on brown paper bags," explains Leverbeck, "inviting the audience to take the bag with them to the exhibition, then fill it

up, and take it home with the art that they wanted." The typeface was OCRK Bold Square, which was screen printed in black, white, and fluorescent pink. The exhibition raised money for the Teenage Cancer Trust through audience voluntary donations in exchange for the art/ideas.

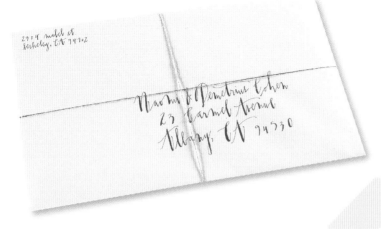

Client: **Kaliyah Eyre**
Design: **Diva Pyari at LINEA CARTA**
Country: **USA**

Kaliyah Eyre baby shower invitation

Pyari designed this invite for the baby shower of Kaliyah Eyre. "The women who commissioned the invite were already familiar with my work and left it up to me to design something fresh," she explains. "Kaliyah was described as bright, joyful, and mindful with a passion for native plants and gardening. I love incorporating nature and organic elements, yet maintaining a clean and modern look, thus the use of my hand-drawn wildflowers and mold-made paper together with a no-frills font." The bright red of the design gives it a modern touch and highlights the wildflower silhouette. After scanning artwork into Photoshop, laying out image and text in Illustrator, and printing a black and white laser copy, Pyari then burned a screen using a Gocco printer and printed each card separately. Each envelope was tied with a delicate nesting twine and sealed with an antique wax seal in white.

Client: **Parent**
Design: **Chris Harman at Parent**
Country: **UK**

Parent promotional card

Parent created this self-promotional card to send to new and prospective clients, and to use at client meetings. The card has been created using a luxurious black Plike (Plastic-Like) stock and all typography has been applied purely using a spot UV varnish. The aim was to play the high-gloss varnish against the rubbery matte feel of Plike. Parent designed the typefaces used on the card. "We often create bespoke typefaces for clients, and wanted to show that off on this promotional card," explains Harman.

Client: **Belinda, S. Chen**
Design: **Belinda, S. Chen**
Country: **UK**

Belinda, S. Chen
business card

After graduating as an illustrator from Central Saint Martins College, London, Chen designed these three business cards using her own illustrations to represent herself and her work. "The illustrations describe what is going on in my head and tell people about my personality and playful mind," explains Chen. The cards have an endearing lo-fi effect as they have been printed on different types of handmade paper.

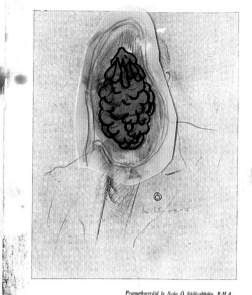

BELINDA,S.CHEN

07817303396

BA0202@HOTMAIL.COM

ILLUSTRATOR

Peannphortráid le Seán Ó Súilleabháin, R.H.A.

Illustrator

BELINDA,S.CHEN

07817303396
ba0202@hotmail.com

IT'S MY IMAGINARY·LAND...

and......
That is.

Belinda, S. Chen
07817303396
ba0202@hotmail.com

Illustrator

Client: **Studio8 Design**
Design: **Studio8 Design**
Country: **UK**

Studio8 Design
business cards

"We wanted the cards to look professional, but not dry and corporate—they needed to have a bit of personality," explains designer Zoë Bather. "And the most important element of the brief was that they needed to be incredibly cheap to produce!" The designers used a high-quality gold foil to apply the type, set in Helvetica Neue, on the basic and free grayboard. The simple, yet bold typography in the gold works well, and in contrast to the lo-fi board. "This is kind of our identity without it really being an 'identity'; simple typography reproduced through interesting and varied printing techniques as on our cards," adds Bather.

Client: **V2 Records**
Design: **GraphicTherapy**
Country: **USA**

V2 Records holiday cards

GraphicTherapy designed these two holiday cards for the V2 record label. The first card was printed on images of scanned black denim, and then buttons were made in the company's brand colors of red and white and pinned to the card. These were mailed in clear cellophane envelopes. The second features red "sausage" balloons manufactured with the tag "Big things come in small packages." This was printed four-color on plastic paper and came with a balloon in a clear cellophane envelope.

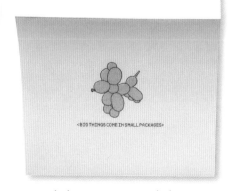

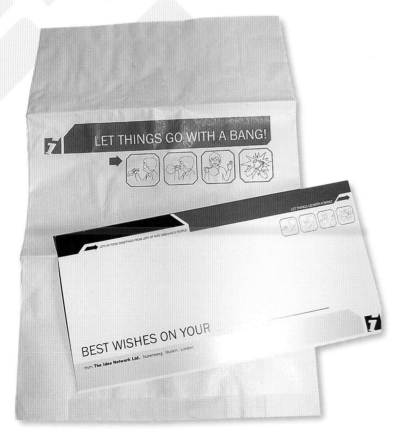

Client: **Ideenhaus**
Design: **Annika Kaltenthaler (AKA)**
Text: **Julian Schäfer**
Country: **Germany**

Big Bang card

This "congratulations" card was designed for customers and friends of Ideenhaus, a brand design agency. The brief was to create a card that could be posted in a normal letter envelope and used not only for birthdays, but also for new jobs, the birth of a baby, etc. "The idea was to create a big bang to have fun with the congratulation," explains Kaltenthaler. "On the card it explains what you have to do, but essentially it is a big bang for your great day." The hand-drawn illustrations were based on the emergency escape cards found on airplanes. Franklin Gothic typeface, the house font of Ideenhaus, has been used throughout.

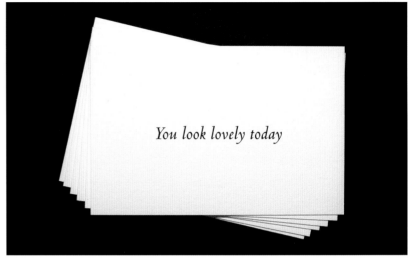

Client: **Keep Calm Gallery**
Design: **Lucas Lepola/Hayley Thwaites
at Keep Calm Gallery**
Country: **UK**

Client: **Studio Oscar**
Design: **Oscar Wilson at Studio Oscar**
Country: **UK**

Oscar Wilson business card

The idea behind the design of this business card was to create a simple, no-nonsense card. The photographic imagery on the front is a detail from "Pirate Pop," a one-off, laser-etched skateboard image also designed by Studio Oscar. The reverse shows the simple application of Wilson's name and contact details, set in straightforward Arial typeface. The card used is matte-laminated on both sides.

You Look Lovely Today business/promotional card

Keep Calm Gallery designed this business/promotional card as a quirky item to sell in packs of 20. They also include one free with every order, so it is the first thing customers see when unwrapping their order. "We just wanted something tactile to give our customers, hopefully making them smile when they opened their package," explains Lepola. "There's not much to the card... it was inspired entirely by one of our favorite phrases, 'You look lovely today.' Because the focus was to be on the phrase, we didn't want any other design feature getting in the way." Although small and simple, the card had to be of high quality to reflect the rest of the Keep Calm products, so it was produced using traditional letterpress printing. A delicate typeface, which works well with the white laid stock, has been used.

Conor
Nolan

CONOR&DAVID
24 South William Street
Dublin 2, Ireland

+353 1 6709333
conor@conoranddavid.com
www.conoranddavid.com

David
Wall

CONOR&DAVID
24 South William Street
Dublin 2, Ireland

+353 1 6709333
david@conoranddavid.com
www.conoranddavid.com

Client: **Turnbull Grey**
Design: **Chris Turnbull at Turnbull Grey**
Country: **UK**

Turnbull Grey
Christmas card

Turnbull Grey designed this Christmas card. "We place a lot of emphasis on the 'crafting' of design including papers, printing techniques, and finishes, and as such we usually hand-make our Christmas Cards using our letterpress proofing press," explains Turnbull. "The press size limits us to about A5 (5¾ x 8¼in/148 x 210mm) or smaller, so the size is dictated by that, and although letterpress printing is perceived to be traditional, we wanted to make something that was contemporary in design." The card has been printed in silver ink on a 350gsm smooth uncoated paper stock. Cooper Black typeface is used because of "its gentle curves and billowy feel, like soft snow falling on roofs," according to Turnbull.

Client: **Conor & David**
Design: **Conor Nolan/David Wall**
      at Conor & David
Country: **Ireland**

Conor & David
business card

When Nolan and Wall formed their graphic design business Conor & David, they wanted to create business cards that had clarity and simplicity with functional elegance. "These are values that we hope to bring to all our design work, so it was appropriate that we should apply them to our own cards," explains Wall. They have achieved this with a simple yet classic typographic design that uses Helvetica Neue for their names, complemented by the elegant Adobe Garamond for the remaining text. The cards have been foil-blocked white on matte black card.

Client: **Herbario**
Art Direction: **Alejandro Posada**
    at **Cuartopiso**
Design: **Carlos J. Roldán at Cuartopiso**
Country: **Colombia**

Herbario business cards

Posada and Roldan designed these business cards for the owners of Herbario, a restaurant in Medellín. The brief was to create something classic and traditional, yet contemporary. "It had to relate to the architecture of the restaurant, which is built mainly of raw, unaltered materials and has botanical-inspired environmental graphics within it," explains Roldan. The front simply shows the restaurant's name and logo, which Posada designed using Tivoli typeface. The reverse has the restaurant's contact details. The card, printed on an uncoated stock, exploits its texture to obtain a vintage look.

Client: **TBA+D (Tom Brown Art+Design)**
Design: **Tom Brown at TBA+D**
Country: **Canada**

TBA+D business card

Brown created a business card for his own studio TBA+D, which designs magazines and creates branding and identities for a range of individuals, products, and corporations. "I wanted to make something that broke down my client's idea of me and what my studio is capable of," he explains. "I wanted something long-lasting and unexpected, and thought, 'why not metal?'" Akzidenz Grotesk typeface has been used to set the text, which was applied to the metal card through etching and drilling.

Client: **Carrot Ltd.**
Design: **Zoë Bather at Studio8 Design/**
Brad Yendle at Design Typography
Country: **UK**

10 Unity Street Gummed book of postcards

Studio8 and Design Typography designed the promotional brochure (a gummed book of postcards) for 10 Unity Street, a residential development involving the refurbishment of a Victorian Gothic college. The owners wanted a high-quality brochure that communicated the balance between the historical facade of the building and its contemporary interior refurbishment. "The gummed binding created a brochure that was more approachable and less 'serious' than the usual corporate development brochures," explains Bather. "The cards could be read in sequence as a book, but also torn out." Extra cards were printed—some were used as compliments slips, others in a second edition of the brochure along with new cards created for the second stage of the development. The card cover has a die-cut logo and is on black Colorplan stock. Lightweight green Colorplan was used for the end-papers together with a heavyweight grayboard back cover. The brochure is gum-bound with a spine edge covered in black binding tape, and then presented in an A6 (4 x 5¾in/105 x 148mm) box with lid—covered in black Colorplan with gloss black foil-blocked logo.

Client: **Absolut Vodka**
Design: **Chris Gray at LOVE**
Country: **UK**

Absolut Disco invitation

Gray created this invite for a Studio 54 themed roller disco celebrating the launch of the limited-edition Absolut Mirror Ball bottle. "I wanted to keep the design simple and elegant to sit properly with the Absolut brand, but also inject some of the color and flavor of the Studio 54 style into it," explains Gray. The design relies primarily on the production techniques used in its construction: mirror-ball card, with holographic foil blocking for the type, and on the reverse debossing to apply the iconic Absolut vodka bottle silhouette. Futura typeface has been used throughout.

Client: **Mass Productions**
Design: **Brad Kayal**
Country: **USA**

Mass Productions business card

Mass Productions is an upstart initiative that promotes and assists filmmaking and production in Massachusetts. Kayal designed the business card shown here as part of its overall identity. "The timing between receiving this project and when I needed to have a file ready for printing was a matter of days," explains Kayal. "In a way I liked having a tight deadline with this project... as for the idea, the client is located in Massachusetts so I wanted to include it in the design somehow." The card features the outline of the state of Massachusetts being held up by an illustration of a tripod. This icon has since become the identity for the whole company. The typeface is Berthold City Medium, and the cards have been printed on an uncoated stock and given slightly rounded corners.

RON LAWNER

PRINCIPAL

535 BOYLSTON STREET, 8TH FLOOR
DIRECT:617.797.0909 FAX:617.267.3166
RON@MASSPRODUCTIONSLLC.COM

MASS PRODUCTIONS

Alissa Morris
Office Manager
alissa@turnstylestudio.com

2219 NW Market Street
Seattle, WA 98107

Client: **Turnstyle**
Art Direction: **Steve Watson at Turnstyle**
Design: **Madeleine Eiche at Turnstyle**
Country: **USA**

Turnstyle business cards

Turnstyle's Eiche created this card with the brief to make it thick, tactile, and readable. "Our last business cards were blind-embossed, which provoked a lot of comment from the people we gave them to," explains Watson. "If nothing else, they were very memorable. We wanted our updated cards to be equally tactile and memorable, but more readable, hence the super-thick three-ply card that allows us to put a deboss and an emboss back-to-back." Orange (Turnstyle studio color) ink has been used with Watson's custom-drawn font.

Client: **Guy Carpenter**
Design: **Chris Turnbull at Turnbull Grey**
Country: **UK**

Space Party invitation

Each year Turnbull Grey creates party invitations following a particular theme (here it was "space") for Guy Carpenter, a global reinsurance company. "The brief was to design an invitation for the party. It would be desk-dropped to staff, and always tends to be a bit gimmicky and fun," explains Turnbull. "It hints at the theme of the party, but nobody knows exactly what the theme is until they arrive." The design imitated the freeze-dried food packets that astronauts use; hence the silver packaging holds the invite and a packet of Haribo Starmix candies. The rocket artwork on the package was created from a photograph of Thunderbird 1 and works well with the use of Helvetica typeface. The package was screenprinted in red onto a silver envelope, while the A6 (4 x 5¾in/105 x 148mm) invite was printed using silver and red with a gloss laminate.

Client: **Alexis Tjian/Robert Madison**
Design: **Diva Pyari at LINEA CARTA**
Country: **USA**

Dahlia wedding invitation set

"I worked with Alexis, the bride-to-be, on this invitation set," explains Pyari. "She wanted to include my illustration and an element of my calligraphy." The bride also chose the color palette—chocolate brown and bee—with the theme of dahlias (her favorite flowers). "I love incorporating organic elements, yet maintaining a clean and modern look, hence the use of my hand-drawn dahlias and hand lettering together with a no-frills font and bright white Lettra paper," she adds. Pyari used Myriad typeface, which pairs well with her "messy" illustration style. Each set was tied with a lime-green string.

Client: **Ayumi K. Piland**
Design: **Ayumi K. Piland at APAK Studio**
Country: **USA**

Handmade greetings cards

"When I began my freelance illustration career, I decided to follow my passion and give myself a fun project," explains Piland. "I invested in a Japanese screen-printing kit called Gocco, and used it to make these notecards. So far I have designed 14. These have been used to send love from one person to another, and at the same time have been a great way to get my work seen."

Piland designed some cards specifically for friends—for example, "Alive" was for the birth of a friend's baby. Others have themes such as "giving," "innocence," "love," and "sharing." "I hope to make something that makes people smile when they see my work," adds Piland. "That's really the main goal of this project." Piland uses recycled paper to create the cards.

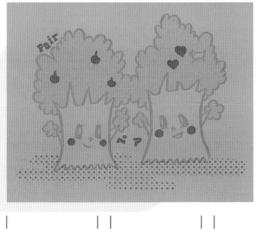

Client: **Christina Föllmer**
Design: **Christina Föllmer**
Country: **Germany**

Stitched greetings cards

Föllmer uses her sewing and embroidery to create these cards. "Whether I work in a free, abstract way or in a figurative way, I express myself through this creativity," she explains. "Often I don't start with a concept or plan; it develops while I work with the thread, experimenting as I go." She sews both by hand and machine, applying her technique to different stocks

and materials, from card to plastic to leaves. The leaf card is a souvenir of a nice day in Hamburg, and the heart card she made for her sister. "I love to express my personality through my sewing," she adds. "I like to create things you can touch, with interesting materials, and I love handmade, charming things that are one of a kind."

Client: **Bronwyn Hughes/Ren Bates**
Design: **Diva Pyari at LINEA CARTA**
Country: **USA**

Ostrich wedding invitation set

Pyari designed this wedding invitation set around the wedding venue's pet ostrich, which the bride and groom fell in love with when they saw it. "I'm inspired by nature, organic textures, and a mixture of hand-drawn sketches with clean fonts and color," explains Pyari. "The Save the Date is an original illustration of an ostrich feather. I love how this image evokes grass—perfect for the outdoor wedding in northern California." Pyari created all the illustration, design, and calligraphy on the set, and used Myriad typeface for its clean, modern look, which complements her "messy" illustration style. She screenprinted each card on a textured stock, and tied each set in packing string. The guest's names and addresses were applied in calligraphy.

Client: **Larry Thompson/Ringling College of Art and Design**
Art Direction: **Jennifer Mumford/ Holly Antoszewski**
Design: **Elsa Chaves**
Country: **USA**

Ringling President's holiday card

The brief for this card was for it to be nondenominational, but festive, and for it to reflect the college's location and Ringling as an art school. "I have always loved origami, and wanted to be able to use it somehow," explains Chaves. "I also wanted the card to be interactive, for the recipient to be able to make something of their own and take part in the creative process. I used the dove, which had been used very successfully in years past, and included orange blossoms, the Florida state flower, as a reference to cherry blossoms." The card includes a two-color vellum sheet of instructions on how to fold an origami dove. The pattern on the vellum insert is an orange blossom, which Chaves created together with all the other illustrations on the card. The card was printed on a coated matte stock.

Client: **Lello**
Design: **Steve Watson at Turnstyle**
Country: **USA**

Lello business card

Lello, a company that designs both interiors and high-end children's apparel, sets itself apart by using unique textiles not normally associated with clothing. "Starting with the name and logo, we set out to embody a friendly yet sophisticated brand," Watson explains. "As the word 'Lello' rhymes with 'hello,' we wanted the cards to reach out, welcome, and greet the recipient." So the card has a subtle, muted color palette on an uncoated stock. The pink and white elements of the design have been foil-stamped to create a contrasting finish and give the cards an interesting visual and tactile quality. A customized version of Helvetica typeface has been used.

Client: **Clara Courtaigne**
Design: **Clara Courtaigne**
Country: **UK**

Send Me Everlasting Flowers greetings card

Courtaigne created this card for an art book fair held at the Institute of Contemporary Arts in London. "I always feel sad offering flowers to people, as they are perishable," she explains. "Therefore designing this card is a poetic way for me to send everlasting flowers." Courtaigne has photocopied and then silk-screen printed an image of flowers onto an A4 (8¼ x 11¾in/210 x 297mm) sheet of paper, which has then been folded into quarters to create an envelope shape complete with markings for the address and stamp. A bellyband holds it all in place. Courtaigne has used cartridge paper and screenprinted the cards using three colors.

1/30   Clara Courtaigne

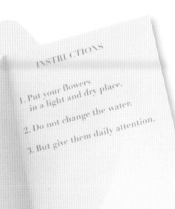

INSTRUCTIONS

1. Put your flowers in a light and dry place.

2. Do not change the water.

3. But give them daily attention.

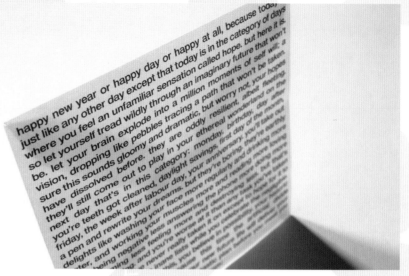

Client: **Karin von Ompteda**
Design: **Karin von Ompteda**
Country: **Canada**

Empty greetings card

"I was interested in designing a New Year greetings card for people who feel pressured into card exchanges for meaningless events," explains von Ompteda. "Abstaining from participation is often the only behavioral option for these people, and I wanted to instead give them a voice. This card was designed for a culture that needs reminding that New Year is just a day, that changing one's behavior is a complex challenge at which most people fail, and which is best not trivialized." A greetings card traditionally contains good wishes. As an empty greeting, von Ompteda was interested in making the card a literal representation of this: a sealed envelope with nothing inside it.

Printing on translucent material was necessary to communicate the card's emptiness. Neue Helvetica BQ has been used throughout the card, digitally printed on architectural semitranslucent vellum. A section at the bottom of each card is reserved for hand-applied sender/sendee personalization.

Client: **The Picture Lounge**
Design: **Andy Mallalieu at Creative Spark**
Country: **UK**

The Picture Lounge business card and invitation

Creative Spark designed this business card and invite for The Picture Lounge, a photographic studio. "The main target audience of the studio is female, so that's why we used a floral illustration on the card and invite," explains Mallalieu. "We wanted to create something classy and elegant." The floral illustration was drawn in-house in Illustrator and set on the card and invite with Minion Regular. Both cards have been matte-laminated on both sides, and feature the use of a metallic gold Pantone color.

Client: **Carmen Marc Valvo**
Design: **GraphicTherapy**
Country: **USA**

Carmen Marc Valvo invitation

GraphicTherapy created the embossed
black invite for the designer's after-party
with the brief to base it on the collection's
central theme—black "Madame X"
couture evening wear. The invite consists
of three pieces of board: the front gloss
black chromalux blind-embossed with
multiple images of the Carmen Marc
Valvo "V" logo pattern, the back letterpress black on uncoated white board,
with both glued to a central board. The
second invitation was for a fall fashion
show. Again this consists of three boards:
the front is brushed stainless-steel
chromalux board blind-embossed, the
back features matte white card which
has been foil-stamped, and both have
been bonded to a central board.

Client: **Graham Mckenzie/Huddersfield Contemporary Music Festival**
Design: **Peter and Paul**
Country: **UK**

HCMF business card

Peter and Paul designed this card for the Huddersfield Contemporary Music Festival (HCMF) artistic director, Graham McKenzie. He wanted a bespoke limited-run card to take to other festivals and give to musicians, funders, and curators. His brief was for the card to have a special quality to make the recipient want to keep it, while upholding the festival's philosophy that "Music lives in everything." This has been achieved by using vinyl. "The idea was to produce a card that somehow created sound," explains Paul Reardon. We bought a batch of random records, laser-etched the graphics on to them and then laser-cut the shape of the card, the idea being that if you scratched the card with a needle it would emit a sound." The utilitarian Franklin Gothic Condensed typeface has been used.

THIS IS A TEST : SAMPLE TEXT. THE QUICK BROWN FOX JUMPED OVER THE LAZY DOG. The quick brown fox jumped over the lazy dog. THE QUICK BROWN FOX JUMPED OVER THE LAZY DOG. The quick brown fox jumped over the lazy dog.

Visual Artist / Designer
Malcom Clarke / mc@malcomclarke.com / +44 (0)7888 729650

A Graphologist's analysis of my handwriting: This is a very individual and personal writing and doesn't come from any copybook style. Therefore you are your own person and do things your own way. Being different is quite important to you. You need the stimulus of being independent and free from control by others, but you also need to have parameters that others will provide, or you won't reach your full potential. You try to find your truths without necessarily worrying about social conventions, not to be confrontational, but because you like to feel free to make up your mind. You are both resourceful and intelligent, but need a reason to be so. Your spiritual area is strong and it shows that you have a conceptual power, the ability to think beyond the obvious and to aspire to goals and ambitions that seem worthwhile to you. Your signature reinforces the information above: that you want to be special and different by setting high standards. You have all the potential, but there is frustration shown with the triangles that appear in the middle zone of your letter 't', showing that often tasks are not satisfying or enjoyable. Your powers of observation are well defined and the issue is with your openness to change that is initiated by other's needs, rather than yours.

Client: **Malcom Clarke**
Design: **Malcom Clarke at Studio MC**
Country: **UK**

Who am I 1.0 business card

Clarke used a conceptual approach to design his business card. "I was looking for a way of expressing a meaning/useful identity, while wanting an authority to execute an assumption of who I am, rather than though my own idea of who I am," explains Clarke. "I decided to focus on handwriting. This has always been used as a true sign of identity, required to authenticate and ratify documents, so it seemed the logical route to explore." Clarke had his handwriting analyzed by a graphologist, and tried to summarize the results on his business card using samples of his handwriting. "It's a way of introducing myself through someone else's cold reading of me," he adds. "I found the idea interesting and will continue to investigate approaches to portraying myself." All other text is set in Rockwell and Rockwell Light because of its good legibility at small point sizes. The cards were printed on Fedrigoni 350gsm Bianco Satin.

THIS IS YOUR NEW FAVOURITE BUSINESS CARD! YOU LOVE IT A special card that you really wanted to see today. The perfect idea, applied with the most deftly crafted typography upon the stock of your dreams. You'll never forget it.

Visual Artist / Designer
Malcom Clarke / mc@malcomclarke.com / +44 (0)7888 729650

"A successful promotional card makes you stop and engage with the object, whether that's because of the concept, the execution of the design, the feel of the materials, or the production techniques."

Chris Turnbull, UK

Client: **Total Content**
Art Direction: **Alan Dye/Ben Stott/**
   Nick Finney at NB: Studio
Design: **Daniel Lock at NB: Studio**
Country: **UK**

Total Content stationery set

Total Content, a copywriting team that works primarily in the art and design sector, commissioned NB: Studio to create its complete stationery set. As well as having a coherent look across all of the individual items, the design needed to be striking and impactful. "The design took its cue from the company name and features the total contents of a copywriter's most basic everyday tool—the alphabet," explains Stott. "In order to illustrate the crafting of words, character and punctuation symbols were placed in a variety of different fonts to reflect the different personalities and styles of their writing. This acted as a visual device to carry through to the different elements of the stationery set that is decorative, descriptive, and encapsulates the coalescence of writing and design." The typograpy was created using a letterpress to give each item an individual, personal, handcrafted feel. Fluorescent orange ink was used to reflect the writers' Dutch heritage. For the smaller stationery items, the design was split up to create three different compliment slips and eight different business cards which, when all placed together again, create the total contents of the alphabet.

Deborah Kings.

totalcontent. Studio The Abbey Warwick Road Southam Warwickshire United Kingdom CV47 0HN
T +01926 812286 M +07870 751958 F +01926 811386
deb@totalcontent.co.uk www.totalcontent.co.uk

totalcontent. Studio The Abbey Warwick Road Southam Warwickshire United Kingdom CV47 0HN
T +01926 812286 M +07976 160967 F +01926 811386 jim@totalcontent.co.uk www.totalcontent.co.uk

VAT No. 786 3716 85

Deborah Kings.

totalcontent. Studio The Abbey Warwick Road
Southam Warwickshire United Kingdom CV47 0HN
T +01926 812286 M +07870 751958 F +01926 811386
deb@totalcontent.co.uk www.totalcontent.co.uk

totalcontent. Studio The Abbey Warwick Road
Southam Warwickshire United Kingdom CV47 0HN

Client: **4Design**
Design: **Deuce Design**
Country: **Australia**

4Design business card

Deuce Design designed the card as part of the overall rebranding and identity package for one of Sydney's leading industrial design firms, 4Design. "The directors of 4Design are edgy and committed to the design process and design in general," explains designer Maggie Tang. "They knew what they wanted, but also encouraged us to bring something new to the identity. The idea was to create an easily recognizable, clean, 3D logo that incorporated the number '4' and the letter 'D.' It had to be green and black as a reference to their former identity, but also had to have a utilitarian, almost transport influence, as though it was stamped on the side of a shipping container." The card was printed using a double hit of fluoro green ink and gloss black foil stamping.

4DESIGN

PRODUCT — ENVIRONMENT — GRAPHIC — MULTIMEDIA
L1/83 FOVEAUX ST / SURRY HILLS NSW 2010 AUSTRALIA
T +612 **9280 4454** / F +612 9280 4655 / 4DESIGN.COM.AU

DIRECTOR

LEE LISTON
M 0404 074 344
LEE@4DESIGN.COM.AU

Client: **Matthew Burvill**
Design: **Matthew Burvill at House Of Burvo**
Country: **UK**

Random Greetings Generator (RGGEN) cards

Burvill's concept for the cards shown here was originally for a competition, but actually developed as a personal, self-promotional piece. "Designing this greetings card gave me the perfect opportunity to use the same scratch-off inks used in lottery cards, which fulfilled the ambition for something 'crafted,'" explains Burvill. "The design also lent itself to a pure typographic design, with the option of scratching in your own personal imagery in the final panel." This forms the random greeting idea so that the sender can customize the card. "In addition to the design of the card, it had to be acceptable within all cultures and religions," he explains. "It meant no 'Christmassy' imagery or language could be used, which is why the card is so anonymous and clinical." The first section of the card contains the option to scratch off Merry, Happy, Joyous, Fantastic, and Delightful, and the second Celebration, Festivity, New Year, Season, and Holiday. The ink used to create the scratch-off panels is an opaque printing ink.

Client: **Kate Goldsworthy**
Design: **Chris Turnbull at Turnbull Grey**
Country: **UK**

Kate Goldsworthy
wedding invitation

Turnbull Grey designed this wedding
invitation package (wedding invitation,
reply card, and business card) for textile
designer Kate Goldsworthy. "The card
had to be earthy, tactile, and relatively
low-key in impact," explains Turnbull.
"Cost was an issue too, so we chose
a utilitarian Dutch grayboard, which
screenprints nicely." To introduce a
special element, an optically variable
metallic ink, which changes from
silver to gold when the card is tilted,
has been used. The printed text in
Rockwell typeface has been reversed
out of a larger block of solid color.

Client: **Deuce Design**
Design: **Deuce Design**
Country: **Australia**

Deuce Design business cards

Deuce Design created its set of business cards to reflect its unique aesthetic. They had to be bold, bright, and decorative. "We wanted more-is-more! Typesetting, icons, patterns, the in-house dog mascot, humor, patterns, and personality have all been included within the design," explains designer Maggie Tang. "The eight cards all work in isolation or as one large puzzle. When you have all the cards (the whole team), you can flip them over and try to match them up. The complete puzzle features a Boston terrier, a handshake, subliminal design messages, and a few studio jokes. The idea was to represent the notion that design and designers work both in isolation and together, and often as consultants." Akkurat typeface has been used on the cards, which have been four-color printed with fluoro inks in place of the normal cyan, magenta, and yellow.

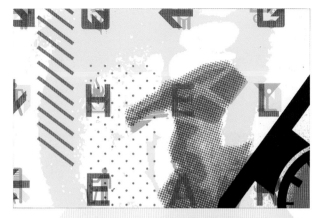

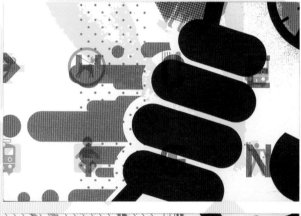

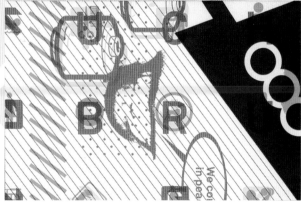

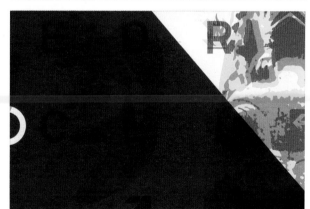

Bruce
from Deuce

Deuce Design
Suite 67
61 Marlborough Street
Surry Hills NSW 2010
Australia

Bruce Slorach
Director

Telephone +61 (0)2 **9699 9710**
Facsimile +61 (0)2 9699 9712
deucedesign.com.au

Mobile +61 (0)418 279 425
bruce@deucedesign.com.au

Client: **Kristina Bowers**
Design: **Kristina Bowers**
Country: **UK**

Kristina Bowers business card

"The challenging part of this project was that I had to set myself a brief, and decide how I wanted to represent myself," explains Bowers. "The main idea was to keep the cards very simple, but also keep them relevant." Bowers has achieved this by leaving the contact information blank so that only her name and website address are on one side of the card. The idea is that the contact details are filled in by hand when she gives out the card so she can always update the cards with new phone numbers, e-mail addresses, etc., without having to get a whole set reprinted. In addition, running from her name one side of the card to the words Graphic Designer on the other is a "linking device" in the form of a dotted line that connects Bowers' name with her occupation. The typeface used throughout is Futura Extra Bold, and the card has been printed using fluorescent pink ink.

Client: **Elastik**
Design: **Damien Aresta at pleaseletmedesign**
Countries: **Belgium/Luxembourg**

Elastik business card

pleaseletmedesign created a logo and business card for web agency Elastik. "We decided to stay very simple with their logo and so just threw an elastic band on our desk and took a picture," explains Aresta. "The logo is at the same time the 'e' of elastik... For the business card, we cut some parts on the sides of the cards on which to place the elastic band around several cards, like a pack of cards. This means that the elastic band is the card holder itself." A fluorescent green ink (Pantone 802C) has been used on one side of the card to represent the pure screen RGB green and its brightness. Storno typeface was used throughout.

Emmanuel Lemal
tel +352 691 943 646 (lu.)
+32 478 94 51 40 (be.)
fax +352 36 60 82

k@elastik.eu
elastik.eu

elastik
the web gymnasts

Client: **Maria Isabel Arango**
Design: **Alejandro Posada at Cuartopiso**
Country: **Colombia**

Maria Isabel & Lucas
wedding invitation

Posada designed this invite for his friend Maria Isabel Arango's marriage to Lucas Ginge. "Her only request was that she wanted an invite that featured swans on it somewhere," explains Posada, "so I used this as a starting point for the design and everything else featured on it just went from there." For the images, Posada created a collage using found imagery and illustrations in old books. He has accompanied the delicate drawings with Dalliance typeface and printed the cards using metallic inks on an uncoated stock.

Client: **University of Applied Sciences Potsdam**
Design: **Svenja von Döhlen at Formdusche**
Country: **Germany**

Innovations Forum Interaktions Design invitation

Formdusche designed this scratch-card invitation for an interaction design conference. Its brief was to communicate interaction through the classic print medium. The key word of the "This is" phrase is hidden under scratch-off ink. The recipient has to interact with the card by using a coin to scratch off the layer of ink to reveal it. FF Magda Clean typeface (Innovations Forum Interaktions Design's corporate font) was used throughout.

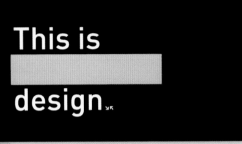

Client: **100% International Dust**
Design: **Steffen Wierer/Svenja von Döhlen at Formdusche**
Country: **Germany**

100% International Dust business card

Formdusche created this card for fashion label 100% International Dust for use on its notes, pricing, and promotion within its packaging. Dust.inc typeface, specially created for 100% International Dust, has been used throughout. Its design was inspired by the billboard typefaces of the 1920s. Gold ink as spot color has also been used on the card.

Client: **NB: Studio**
Art Direction: **Alan Dye/Ben Stott/**
   Nick Finney at NB: Studio
Design: **Jodie Wightman at NB: Studio**
Illustration: **James Graham**
Copywriting: **Vivienne Hamilton**
Country: **UK**

Monsters Ink book and invitation

NB: Studio created the Monsters Ink book and invite project shown here for its Halloween party. The book was a giveaway at the event and also acted as a promotional piece for Hamilton and Graham. "In the interest of 'feeling the fear and doing it anyway,' we brought together an indispensable guide within the book to all that's ghastly, misshapen, ghoulish, and hideaous," explains Stott. "After researching mythical monsters in different cultures, we commissioned James Graham to illustrate a selected few in his eccentric and eclectic hand-drawn style, which we then featured in the book." Text and images were screenprinted in white onto black paper using glow-in-the-dark ink to give the book a contrasting and dark feel.

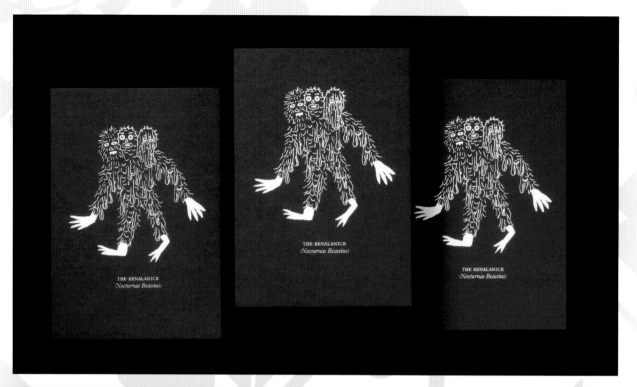

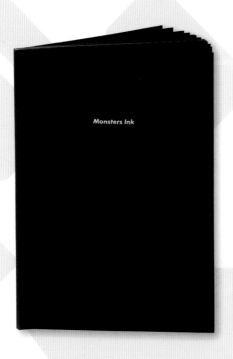

Monsters Ink

Originally very beautiful women transformed into hideously ugly monsters, **Gorgons** are identified by the crown of writhing live snakes on their heads. Noted in many classical Greek texts as Queens of the Underworld, their additional features include a round flat face, lolling tongue and sometimes the tusks of a boar. The most famous example of this fearsome creature is undoubtedly Medusa, who, like her sisters, could turn onlookers into stone.

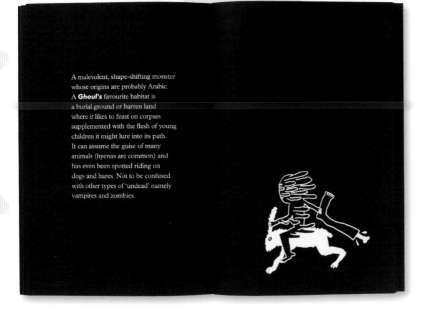

A malevolent, shape-shifting monster whose origins are probably Arabic. A **Ghoul's** favourite habitat is a burial ground or barren land where it likes to feast on corpses supplemented with the flesh of young children it might lure into its path. It can assume the guise of many animals (hyenas are common) and has even been spotted riding on dogs and hares. Not to be confused with other types of 'undead' namely vampires and zombies.

A monstrous race of super-strong huge beings as tall as mountains with shaggy hair and dragon scales on their feet. From Scandinavia to Eastern Europe all **Giants** are typified by a remarkable stupidity with a penchant for tossing boulders and cannibalism. Although fierce, if encountered their intellectual incompetence offers intended victims a good chance of survival by outwitting them.

Client: **Larissa Marquez**
Design: **Tatiana Arocha**
Country: **USA**

Flavio & Larissa
wedding invitation

Arocha designed this wedding invite for her best friend, Larissa Marquez. "She had seen other wedding invitations I had done, as well as my artwork, and wanted something similar for her wedding," explains Arocha. Tropical flowers and Marquez's wedding hair-decoration flowers inspired the design. "I borrowed the flowers from an antique Japanese book of floral patterns I found in Kyoto because that had the delicate, bold look I wanted," adds Arocha. The use of tropical-looking flowers and one ink gives the card a beautiful simplicity. The cards were printed using a letterpress and Emily typeface was used throughout.

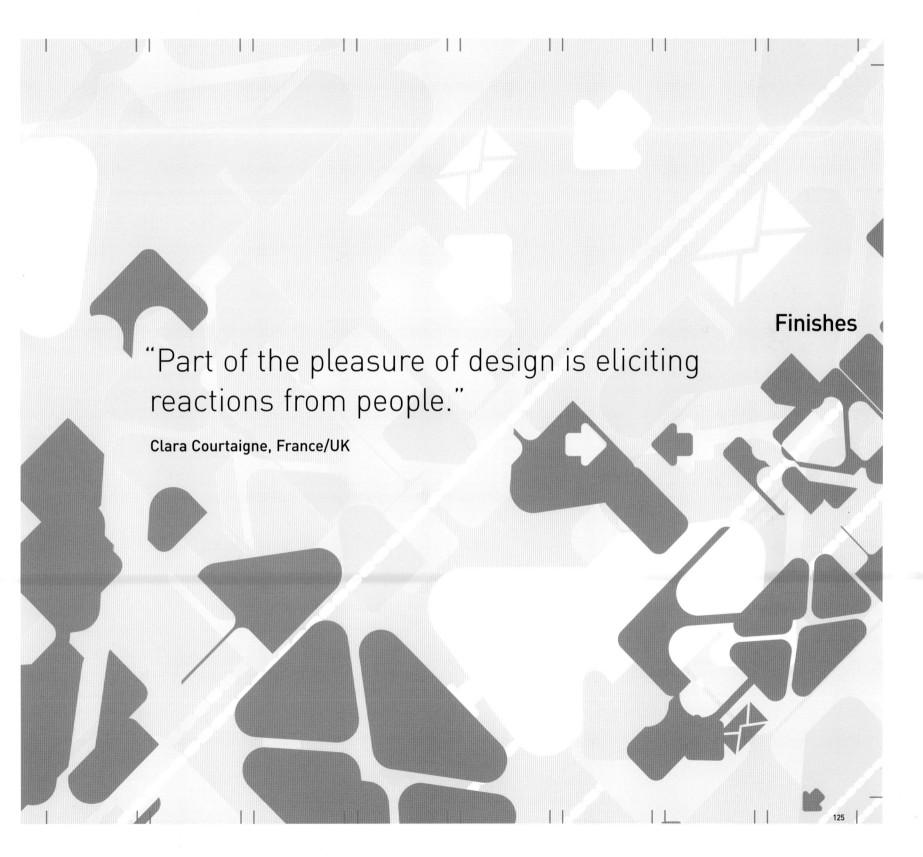

"Part of the pleasure of design is eliciting reactions from people."

Clara Courtaigne, France/UK

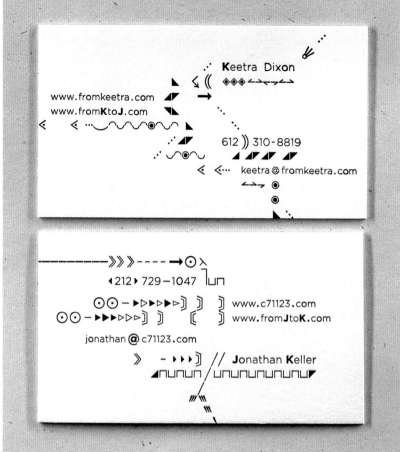

Client: **FromJtoK/FromKtoJ**
Design: **Jonathan Keller**
Print: **Kiyotaka Matsumoto/Letterpress 77**
Countries: **Germany/USA**

Letterpress spam cards, business cards, and postcard

Keller designed these cards for himself (FromJtoK) and Keetra Dean Dixon (FromKtoJ). The duo specializes in 2D and 3D design, focusing on non-commissioned work, but occasionally finds the "lure of a shiny client job too seductive to resist." The idea was to design business cards (and also a postcard) for the duo using letterpress.

Japanese spam, received via e-mail by Keller, and the Unicode character set inspired the card imagery. Gotham typeface has been used for all other text, as its correct weight variations and circularity fit well with the Unicode shapes. Four-color letterpress has been used, with one ink-free pass.

Client: **Emmi**
Design: **Emmi Salonen at Emmi**
Country: **UK**

Take Note badge card

"Notepaper is a personal fascination
of mine, which is also demonstrated
through a number of items designed by
my studio," explains Salonen. "Combining
this with the love for badges was natural
and this is the way the 'take note' series
came about." The idea was to create
notepapers that have been made into
badges and packaged like notebooks
on a small scale, and use them as self-
promotional tools. "As with most of the
badges I design, I like to take the design
of the badge and build a packaging
around it, pushing the theme even
further," adds Salonen. "The notebook
idea is considered throughout, even on
 the spine of the 'notebook' with a smaller
than usual-sized stapling." The text on
the reverse is set in Courier. "It felt
suitable for an item that plays with
the idea of writing," explains Salonen.

Client: **Emmi**
Design: **Emmi Salonen at Emmi**
Country: **UK**

Home Is... badge card

"This badge was a result of the love for
our studio record player and the time
spent working in the studio," explains
Salonen. "I wanted to sell these badges
in various shops, so packaging it with the
record-player graphics and in a plastic
bag seemed a natural option—it protects
the product and reinforces the idea."
The badge packaging relates to the action
of listening to vinyl records—how a user
takes them out of their sleeves, and
turns them over to play the other side.
The imagery is an illustration of the top
of a record player with a line pattern in
the background, designed by Salonen.
"I wanted to have fun with the packaging
and in a way turn the badge into a record,
sitting on a player," adds Salonen. The
badge was sold in specialist design
bookstores across Europe.

Client: **Milkcrate Event Management Group**
Design: **Liam Johnstone/Garus Booth**
Country: **Canada**

Milkcrate Event Management Group business card

Johnstone and Booth focused on Milkcrate's multifaceted abilities for this business card and branding. "They wanted us to create a card that was playful and memorable, yet still had a professional look," explains Johnstone. "They wanted prospective clients to know that they could go to them for any kind of event imaginable, from weddings to birthdays to concerts, so they chose 'Milkcrate' for this very reason. Aside from being a friendly name, it also spoke of versatility," adds Johnstone. "I have never actually seen a milk crate used to

hold milk, but I have seen it hold records, be used as seating or a bookshelf, and we carried this whole idea through to the card." The front shows the company name and web address and is die-cut into the shape of a milk crate with the handle at the top. The flip side shows the individual's personal contact info, with the die-cut milk crate upside down. The logo typeface, a custom font created by Johnstone and Booth, was cut from linoleum-block, then printed, scanned, adjusted in Photoshop, and finally vectorized and colored in Illustrator.

Client: **Kate Banazi**
Design: **Kate Banazi**
Countries: **Australia/UK**

Pyramid greetings cards

Banazi created these 3D greetings cards. Some were to be given away free with purchases of her prints, others sold, and some sent out with packages to agencies to promote her work. "I wanted them to be non-event-specific, so as to be able to be used for any event," explains Banazi. "The pyramid cards came about as a potential alternative to Christmas cards, but without being so festive that they couldn't be used at another time of year." Each of the cards has been silk-screen printed by hand with silver or gold stars.

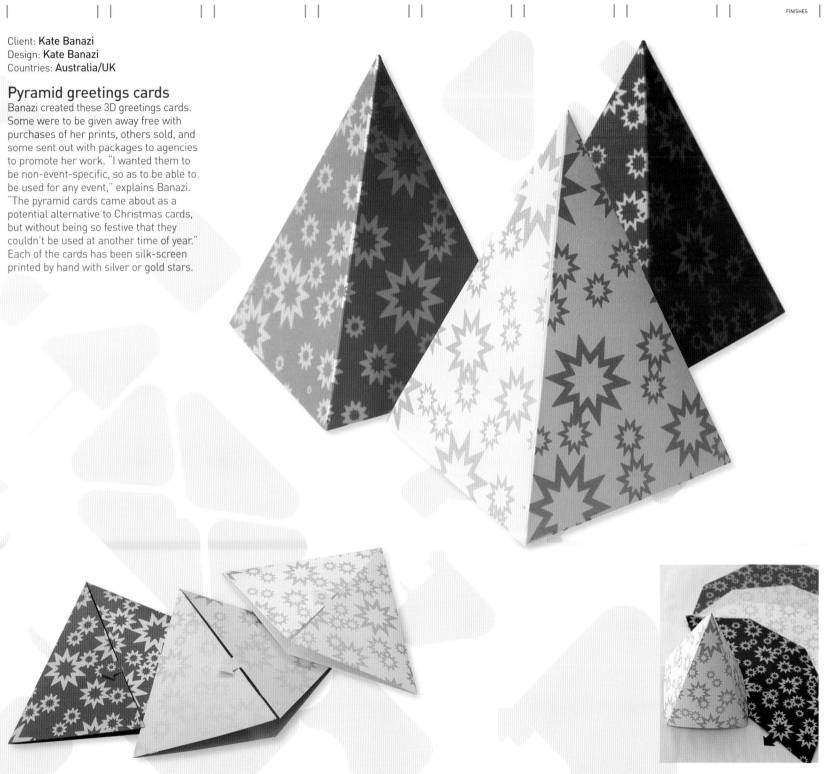

Client: **Nicholas Felton**
Design: **Nicholas Felton**
Country: **USA**

Nicholas Felton change-of-address postcards

Felton designed these cards to inform his friends and family that he was moving house. "By creating an adhesive announcement, I was able to customize and repurpose old postcards to create the announcement," he explains. "Much of my personal work is an outlet of what interests me the most at the time of creation. In this case, I was exploring tightly ruled linear compositions in my sketchbooks and decided they could work well as a backdrop for my new address." Felton created the imagery used for the packing tape, while the postcard imagery comes from numerous sources within his own collection, including the illustration work of Danielle Huthart, old postcards, promotions, and advertising. "I wanted to reuse a range of cards, and also to ensure that all the announcements were different," he adds. Felton has used VAG Rounded throughout, and translucent white packing tape imprinted with black ink in a 12in (30cm) repeating pattern.

Client: **Lowe Counsel**
Design: **Mike Peck**
Countries: **UK/USA**

Lowe Counsel business cards

Peck created an identity and business cards for Lowe Counsel, a leading-edge trends and research consultancy. Peck used photographic imagery supplied by Counsel to create a series of cards with random and often abstract images on the reverse of each card, complemented by the subtle die-cut "o" in the name "Counsel." The design concept means that each card is unique—and there are over 120 variations.

counsel

charlotte rivers \ research network manager
lowe worldwide \ 60 sloane avenue, london, sw3 3xb
+44 207 894 5929 \ charlotte.rivers@loweworldwide.com
www.lowecounsel.com

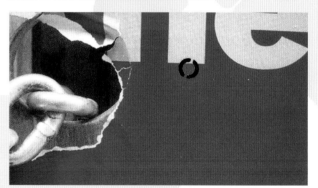

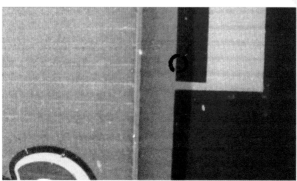

Client: **Giant Artists**
Design: **GraphicTherapy**
Country: **USA**

Giant Artists
promotional cards

GraphicTherapy designed these 45 cards
to showcase individual artists on the
Giant Artists roster. The brief was to
make something special, but not too
expensive, that could be sent out to
prospective clients. The solution was
to wrap the cards in light gray French
board that has been blind-embossed
with repeat circular motifs. The "pack"
has then been bound together with a
black silicone rubber band. The company
logo has been silk-screened on the back
and each pack was mailed in a clear
cellophane envelope.

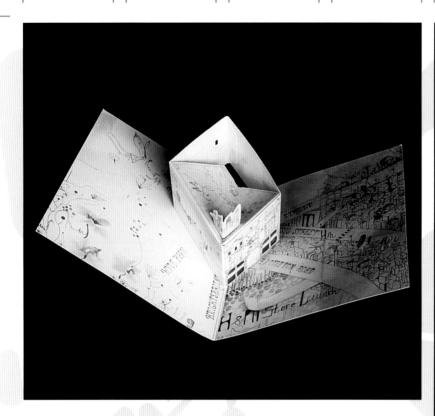

Client: **H&M**
Design: **Simon Glover at ODD**
Illustration: **David Bray**
Country: **UK**

H&M store launch invitation

ODD designed the press-night invite for the launch event of H&M's new flagship store in London. This invite needed to stamp H&M's authority as a fashion leader. "In a time when pop-up stores featured in many marketing campaigns, we thought we'd use a more literal interpretation and create a pop-up card," explains Glover. "The card was adorned with imagery created by illustrator David Bray, who produced dreamy, seductive scenes to communicate the information about the store and the night." The invitation was made on A4 (8¼ x 11¾in/ 210 x 297mm) card folded down to A5 (5¾ x 8¼in/148 x 210mm), with bespoke die-cutting for the pop-up mechanisms.

EMMI SALONEN

Graphic Designer

hello@emmi.co.uk

www.emmi.co.uk

077 5200 1311

Client: **Emmi**
Design: **Emmi Salonen at Emmi**
Country: **UK**

Emmi business card

This is Salonen's personal business card." I wanted it to be simple and show what I do by creating a reaction when people get it," Salonen explains, "and also reflect the character of the studio." Salonen collects notebooks and has a passion for their simplicity. "The studio doesn't really have a logo, so using a visual element that has the feel of the type of a design studio and style was needed." The hole punch as a finishing touch brings the card alive. "My main problem is the quantity of e-mails asking me to reproduce the card for other people," Salonen says. "I always say no to this request, so I either end up designing a new card for them or never hearing from them again." Emmi's Simple typeface has been used. The card has been exhibited at the Eisner American Museum of Advertising and Design in Milwaukee, USA.

Client: **So Takahashi**
Design: **So Takahashi at Heads Inc.**
Countries: **Norway/USA**

Heads Inc. business card

Takahashi's Heads Inc. specializes in 3D design, packaging, and window display, so when he designed its business card it was important for it to reflect its practice. "Tactility in design is very important to me," explains Takahashi, "so I decided to develop the design with the emphasis on that, so that it was a business card that was remembered not only for how it looked, but also how it felt." This has been achieved by simply applying a different-shaped piece of card on top of the usual-shaped business card. At first glance the card looks like a simple, plain white business card, but on closer inspection the additional shape gives it that 3D appearance.

Client: **Joel Bailey/Petter Eriksson/
Sofia Leverbeck/Magnus Polbratt**
Design: **Sofia Leverbeck/
Magnus Polbratt/Studio-SM**
Country: **UK**

Influences invitation

Leverbeck and Polbratt designed this invite for a one-day exhibition focusing on influences in daily life. "We placed actual yellow frames along Brick Lane (in London) to try to make people more aware of what the influences could be, such as a sticker on the wall or a funnily placed milk carton on the side of the street," explains Leverbeck. "The invite that people received could then be separated into two pieces, one mimicking the yellow frames. The idea was to try to make people use this frame by hanging or placing it around things they took notice of, things they might be influenced by." Baskerville typeface has been used as it works well with the "old school" border decorations used on the invite. The invite was printed letterpress with text in black and border in a mixture of gray and silver ink to create a slight reflection/sparkle when put under a light.

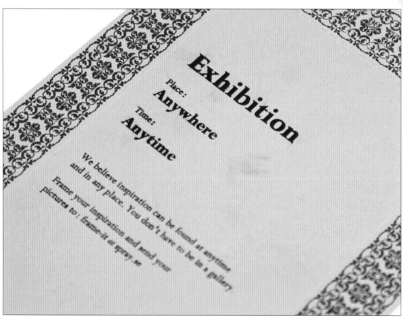

Client: **Formdusche**
Design: **Formdusche**
Country: **Germany**

Formdusche business cards

Formdusche designed its own business cards. The idea was to create one business card for the Formdusche team of four, but somehow make each one individual and specific to each team member. To achieve this, the generic company information is on the front of the card, with the individual cell-phone numbers and portraits being hand-stamped on the reverse to personalize the cards as they are given out. Cholla typeface, as the Formdusche house font, was used throughout.

fd büro für gestaltung // marienburger straße 25 // 10405 berlin // fon 030.47 37 44 77 // fax 030.47 37 44 78 // mobil 0175.886 35 53 // kontakt@formdusche.de // www.formdusche.de

svenja von döhlen
0176.240 320 53

tim finke
0176.23 180 150

steffen wierer
0176.24 032 052

borries schwesinger
0176.24 52 17 29

Client: **University of Brighton**
Design: **James Lunn**
Country: **UK**

School of Historical & Critical Studies invitation

Lunn won the university competition for second-year graphics students to design this invite for the final degree show of Historical & Critical Studies at the University of Brighton. The brief was to highlight the three courses within the school, keep the invite to A5 size (5¾ x 8¼in/148 x 210mm) for ease of posting, and not portray the school as "boring" or overly academic. "The idea was to show the difference in perspective between the three courses by using a random pattern of type and color within the name of the school on the invite," Lunn explains. "I have done this using three different colors within the letters, which I created using a stencil of Century Gothic." By applying the letters with a stencil, Lunn created a letterpress-style finish even though a lithograph printer was used to print the final invite, on GS Smith Vanilla 280gsm.

(A1)
(A2)
(A3)

EDITION LIMITED
A Group Show

Featuring 25 artists & designers
Curation & design by Oscar Bauer

'For some of us rules are a necessity that help us function, and for others rules tie us down and restrict our creativity'

All exhibitors were confronted with a brief and rules that they had to follow; the piece had to be grayscale and a ISO-A format. As well as these they were asked to impose two additional rules upon themselves.

Private View Friday 15th 6–9pm
16th & 17th December, 12–6pm

If possible please wear black, white or grey clothing to the private view. Drinks will be served and live music will be enjoyed.

● TERRACE

4–17 Frederick Terrace
London
E8 4EW

www.terracestudios.co.uk
info@terracestudios.co.uk
07913 681286

Bus: 67, 149, 242, 243

Tube: Liverpool Street, Old Street

Client: **Oscar Bauer**
Design: **Oscar Bauer**
Country: **UK**

Edition Limited flier

Bauer created this flier to promote an exhibition he put together as part of his final research project at Central Saint Martins, London. "The exhibition consisted of 25 artists and designers," explains Bauer. "The rules were that only black and white could be used and all the work had to be in ISO-A sizes. I wanted to show what a few of these rules were within the design.

I also wanted to try to show that there were many participants in the project." Before Bauer distributed it, he bent the top right corner to give the card more of a 3D feel. He printed it in a black-and-white gradient, cut it out, then bent the top right corner over, photographed the layout, and printed it again. He used Giza and Minion typefaces throughout the design.

Client: **So Takahashi**
Design: **So Takahashi at Heads Inc.**
Countries: **Norway/USA**

Heads Inc. Happy Holidays greetings card

Takahashi created this greetings card to give to friends and clients. "Inspired by the candle's flickering flame, I decided to design a candle shade to capture that beauty," explains Takahashi. "3D design is my counterattack on computer-based 2D designs. I am always trying to apply my ideas to different media because

I don't believe in limits in design."
To achieve the production of this 3D card, aircraft-grade birch plywood was used laser-cut. The idea was to create a snow-like feeling within the shade. Instructions on how to use the card were printed on the vellum paper that protected the candle.

"Happy Holidays" Tea Light Candle Shade

Insert tabs from the outside in

Heads Inc. 594 Broadway #1203S New York, NY 10012 T 212 941 5970 F 212 941 6087 e-mail: info@headsinc.com web: www.headsinc.com "Happy Holidays" Tea Light Candle Shade Designed by So Takahashi

Nice Job!

Let it Glow!

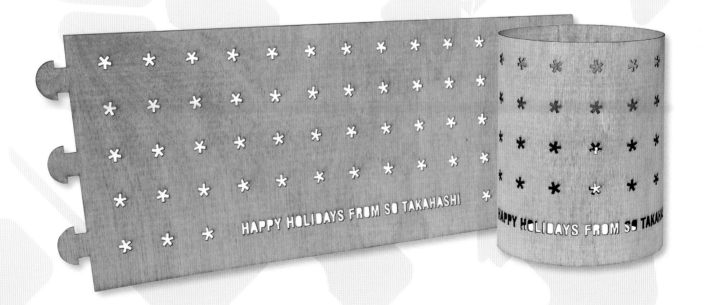

HAPPY HOLIDAYS FROM SO TAKAHASHI

Client: **Kerry Daynes Associates**
Design: **Mark Lester at MARK Studio**
Country: **UK**

Kerry Daynes business card

Kerry Daynes Associates, consultants
in forensic psychology and experts in
criminal profiling and behavioral analysis,
commissioned MARK Studio to create its
identity and subsequent business card.
"With a growing national and international
profile (including TV), Kerry Daynes
(founder of the business) needed an
identity and business cards which would
reflect the business in a simple and
engaging manner," explains Lester.
"The cards needed to be suitably
different, a talking point when received,
something that people would want to
keep, iconic, and simple." Lester took the
idea of a missing piece of the jigsaw,
which also doubles up into the letter "K"
in the company name, to create the logo.
For this business card, the jigsaw/letter
has been laser die-cut out of the card,
which is micron black acrylic plastic.

Client: **Camron PR**
Design: **Daniel Baer at Studio Daniel Baer**
Country: **UK**

Camron PR Christmas card

Baer designed this Christmas card as a limited-edition VIP card for the clients of Camron PR, a leading agency in design, interiors, art, food, and fashion. "I wanted a fresh take on Christmas, using representations, but kept within a modern frame," explains Baer. "The design adopts the style of traditional Victorian Christmas cards, but with a contemporary feel." All the elements of the card are hand-drawn, and the bird shape has been filled with a pattern of Victorian lace. "It gives the bird texture, and the pattern gives shape to the bird's eyes, feathers, and facial expression," he adds. Foil-blocked Big Caslon typeface has been used on the back of the card to add a festive feel.

Season's Greetings & Happy New Year

CAMRON
7 FLORAL STREET • LONDON WC2E 9DH
TELEPHONE +44(0)20 7420 1700 • FAX +44(0)20 7497 2753
WWW.CAMRON.CO.UK

Client: **MARK Studio**
Design: **Mark Lester at MARK Studio**
Country: **UK**

MARK Christmas card

MARK Studio designed this Christmas mailer, which features a pair of socks threaded through a die-cut slot in duplex board and has then been shrink-wrapped. It was sent to clients and friends with the following warning: only to be used in case of a total inspiration failure. "We ironically repackaged a traditional all-purpose Christmas present," explains Lester. "We wanted to create a memorable mailer for our clients and friends." The typeface used is Helvetica Neue.

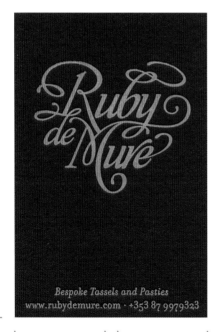

Client: **Ruby de Mure**
Design: **David Wall at Conor & David**
Country: **Ireland**

Ruby de Mure business card

"Ruby wanted us to come up with a design that would sit comfortably alongside her existing paraphernalia, which included the tassels she creates and the handmade boxes in which they are delivered," explains Wall. "Our discussions with Ruby for the project revolved around burlesque imagery—both vintage and contemporary—with which she felt a connection and affiliation. It was agreed at an early stage that the design should be sexy without feeling trashy or cheap. It was about celebrating the feminine form as opposed to exploiting or objectifying it." Conor & David used Affair typeface to create her logo. "Affair was the perfect choice for reasons both aesthetic and practical," explains Wall. "It captured the sense of intrigue and sensuality that we were looking for. The typeface has a formidable array of alternate characters which we customized to fit our needs." The card has been printed using matte foil blocking on matte claret-colored card.

Client: **Magnus Dennis**
Design: **Tim Moore at Nth Creative**
Country: **UK**

Magnus Dennis
business card

Moore designed this business card for photographer Magnus Dennis. "The concept behind the card is to focus on the photographer as a selector of views, an eye for compositional balance, by cutting an aperture/viewfinder that isn't 35mm, but conforms to the proportions of a widescreen film frame and is offset from the center following the golden section proportions," explains Moore. "This idea was to combine Magnus's role as a photographer and cameraman who also works as a producer of film." The card was litho-printed in a deep uncoated Pantone 289, and the viewfinder was die-cut into it. The card text was set in Gill Sans Alt One and follows a grid that is offset from the 16:9 cut frame.

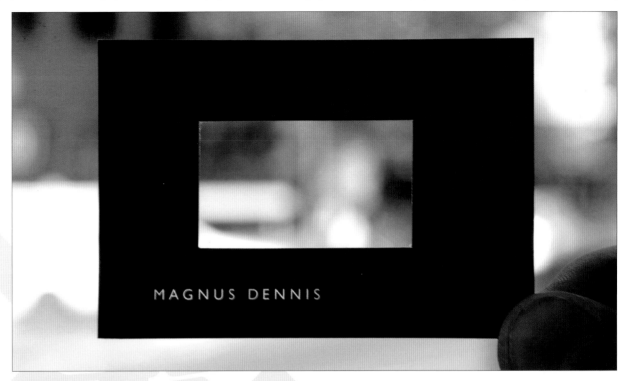

ceo : **Akinori Oishi**

mail to : **ceo@aki-air.com**

web : **http://aki-air.com**

service : **+81 (0) 80 5123 1972**

Client: **Aki-Air.com**
Design: **Akinori Oishi**
Country: **Japan**

Aki Airport business card/sticker

Oishi designed this sticker-style business card for his design company, Aki-Air.com. He works mainly in graphics, animation, interactive design, and web design. His card features his illustrations of a small airport complete with mini-characters. "The reason I chose to use a sticker as my business card is that people love stickers," he explains. "It makes it quite unique, and hopefully something that will be remembered by my clients as well as stuck somewhere so they will always have my contact details."

Client: **Belinda, S. Chen**
Design: **Belinda, S. Chen**
Country: **UK**

Book of Stairs postcards

Chen created these postcards to promote her *Book of Stairs*. "The image on the cards is inspired by stairs that I saw in Roman Baths which lead to nowhere," explains Chen. "And also by my dreams. I think about going up the stairs and them leading me somewhere else, so this postcard is also supposed to represent a dreamlike, utopian spirit." The cards have been silk-screen printed onto different stocks, some coated and some uncoated. They show how a simple concept can be well executed to produce great lo-fi results.

Client: **NB: Studio**
Art Direction: **Alan Dye/Ben Stott/**
　Nick Finney at NB: Studio
Design: **Daniel Lock at NB: Studio**
Country: **UK**

NB: Studio Christmas card

NB: Studio designed this Christmas card and used several interesting printing and finishing techniques. First it created the main body of the card with nine individual pieces of card cut to different lengths. These pieces of card were then Singer-sewn together so that when they are viewed from the side, the card looks like a traditional pine Christmas tree. The inner greeting text was applied in white using screenprinting, and then each card was hand-painted with pine oil to give it a festive scent. All in all it makes a thoughtful, festive, handcrafted card.

Client: **Betti Polk/Harald Martini**
Design: **Annika Kaltenthaler (AKA)**
Country: **Germany**

Betti & Harald
wedding invitation

Kaltenthaler designed this wedding invitation for her friends, Betti and Harald. "My brief was very free," she explains. "They just wanted a nice, sweet, romantic, but special wedding invitation." The invite has been created using five hearts with a message on each one (Betti and Harald, their photograph, the motto, invitation text, and the date).

The envelope also contained some little hearts. On the reverse are illustrations of butterflies and images of nature relating to the wedding venue, an old country mill. American Typewriter and DIN typefaces have been used throughout. The handmade invites were sent out in transparent paper envelopes.

Client: **Ian Anderson/Kari Radasch/ Clifton Burt/Kate Bingaman-Burt**
Design: **Kate Bingaman-Burt/ Public Design Center**
Country: **USA**

Holy Double Matrimony! invitation

When two couples with many mutual friends decided to get married in a double wedding ceremony, an invitation to celebrate the occasion's uniqueness was required. Bingaman-Burt, one half of one of the couples, was given this task. "I like blending the vintage with the new,

and I wanted the invite to give an indication of what to expect from the wedding weekend. It was important to me that it be personal, funny, and well designed." The vintage couples' pictures came from a copyright-free wedding imagery book, the photos were shot in

a photo booth, and Bingaman-Burt hand-drew the text. "We wanted to use a formal vintage illustration and mash it up against illustrated type to create hopefully something that represented the four of us," she adds. The invites were screenprinted.

Client: ±
Design: **Peter Crnokrak at ±**
Country: **UK**

± business card

± created its new identity including this card. "We wanted the card to express the ethos of the studio—modern, minimal, and information-rich," explains Crnokrak. There are two ideas behind the design: minimalist modernism and humanist information design. As such, the 5 × 9 dot-grid side of the card features a single hand-colored dot using graphite pencil. When the card is viewed at a 90-degree angle, the graphite does not show, but when it is tilted to catch the light, the contrast between the metallic graphite finish and the matte paper shows. With only e-mail contact information, the card's design is very clean, while the dot grid and hand-appliqué graphite dot personify the idea of information and the human hand.

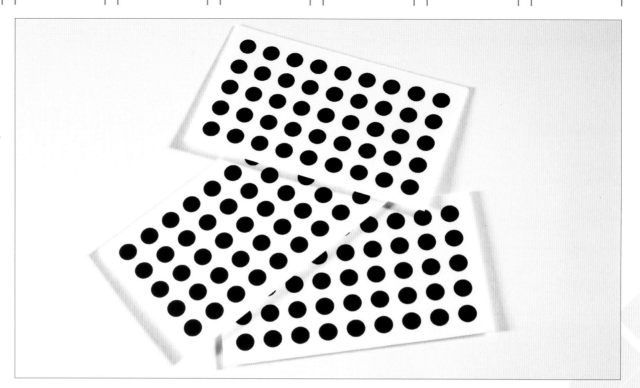

Client: **Gavin Martin Associates**
Art Direction: **Alan Dye/Ben Stott/
Nick Finney at NB: Studio**
Design: **Daniel Lock at NB: Studio**
Country: **UK**

Gavin Martin change-of-address card

NB: Studio designed this piece of direct mail to announce printer Gavin Martin Associates' move to new offices. "Taking cue from their new location, The Tea Building in Shoreditch, we decided to lavishly letterpress the typography onto GF Smith card and then painstakingly hand-stain all 1,000 cards with a tea ring to reflect the idea of removal and removal men leaving tea stains all over the office," explains Lock. It makes a great series of cards that feature letterpress-printed text and stains hand-printed with real tea—substituting cyan, magenta, yellow, and black with Earl Grey, Darjeeling, Rooibos, and English Breakfast teas.

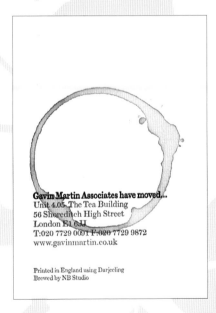

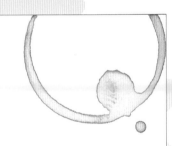

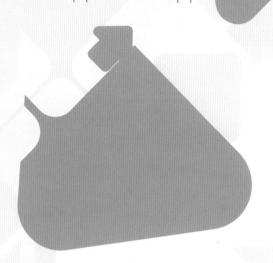

Chris Turnbull, Turnbull Grey, UK

What do you think is the most important thing about creating a business card, invite, or other promo items?
As with all design, the crucial thing is to consider the intention, who the audience is and what it is trying to convey about the event or company sending it. Is it to be fun, frivolous, or something more serious or lavish? The invitation is the ambassador; it needs to communicate something of the occasion or the company that it is announcing/representing.

What are the considerations?
How is the invitation going to be distributed? If posted, will bespoke envelopes be created or does it have to be a standard size? Will its size or weight affect postage costs? Budget: often an invitation is considered to be a lesser priority and an add-on to the event, which is a mistake because it is the invitation that is going to generate the interest and desire to attend the event.

What makes one design successful over another?
Its ability to make you actually stop and engage with the object, whether that's because of the concept, the execution of the design, or the feel of the materials, production techniques, or the construction of the object.

How did you get into design?
I had always drawn, but was a mature student when I studied Fine Art and Graphic Design at Camberwell College of Arts [in London] and specialized in printmaking. Leaving College, I worked as an artist and freelance designer; after a few years, I found my interests shifting more toward graphic design and that became my dominant creative direction. I still make my own work to exhibit when time allows.

What inspires your work in general?
My background as an artist-printmaker is a big influence with regard to the use of papers and production techniques. We have a collection of letterpress type and a small press in the studio, which is always good to play on and use when appropriate. Good design is as much about the tactile as the visual experience. The "crafting" of a piece of design is important to me. Invitations and cards provide a good opportunity for me to explore this area.

What has been your favorite invite project to work on?
The invitations for the University of the Arts London Conferment Ceremonies. These are prestigious events when the University awards Professorships to the likes of Giorgio Armani and Tom Dixon. The invitation is part of a larger branding package for the occasion, which includes brochures and presentation boxes, but the invitation sets the style and tone for the other items.

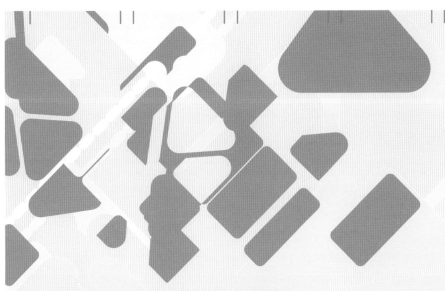

Bruce Slorach, Deuce Design, Australia

What do you think is the most important thing about creating a business card or other communication for a company?
That it communicates the client's intention clearly and within budget. Also, something that surprises the client and exceeds their expectations.

What makes one design successful over another?
Clear, interesting outcomes and design bravery. To some extent breaking the "cookie-cutter mold."

How did you get into design?
I started from an early age. My father was into drawing (life drawing), building models, and bronze sculptures, and we did a lot of this together. Then, when I was 13 I won the Australian Wool Board Poster Competition. From there I did a foundation year in Art and Design, aged 16, at Prahran College [Melbourne] and at 17 I went to the Victorian College of the Arts where I did a Fine Arts degree, majoring in painting and printmaking. Apart from a brief stint as Design Director for another design business, I have always had my own design studio.

What inspires your work?
Art, travel, books, and everydayness. There are millions of designers and artists I really like—too many to name.

You use a lot of illustration in your work; can you explain why that is?
I've spent my life drawing in some capacity. I think an illustrative element can add another layer and dimension.

What are the characters in your illustrations based on?
I have lots of different influences in terms of illustrations, from Australiana to William Morris to Ed Roth and traditional Japanese tattooing. I could go on forever.

What has been your favorite project to work on and why?
Jacaranda Square (at Sydney Olympic Park) and the Sydney Harbour Bridge 75th Anniversary. Both had very good teams, were public projects, and had a certain amount of design freedom. And the client was happy with the design solution.

What would be your dream project to work on and why?
There are a few things that I love to work on: boutique hotels (wallpapers to floors and everything in between...); international exhibition graphics; a book on world signage; and a fantastic way-finding program.

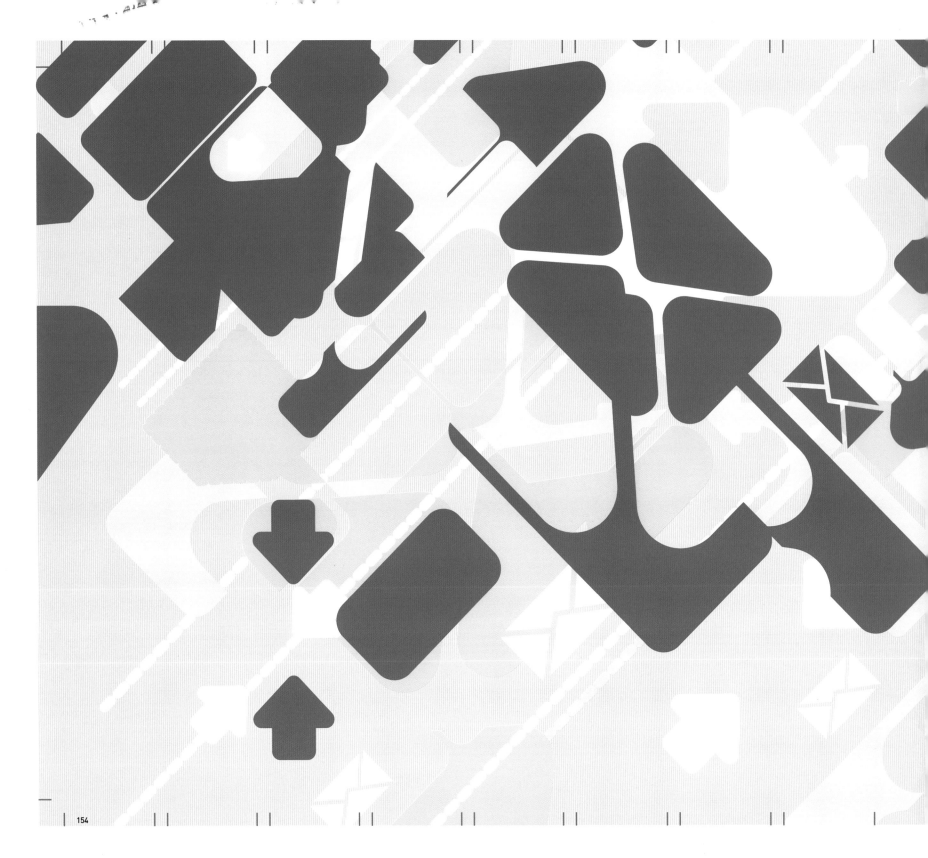

Contact Details & Acknowledgments

Contact Details

Jonathan Keller
www.c71123.com / jk@c71123.com

LAKI 139
www.laki139.com / simon@laki139.com

James Langdon
www.jameslangdonwork.net /
studio@jameslangdonwork.net

Less Rain
www.lessrain.com / carsten@lessrain.com

Katharina Leuzinger (Studio Mielo)
www.katleuzinger.com / mail@katleuzinger.com

LINEA CARTA
www.linea-carta.com / diva@linea-carta.com

Little Oranges (Emily Desai)
www.littleoranges.com / info@littleoranges.com

Lobby Design
www.lobbydesign.se / info@lobbydesign.se

LOVE
www.lovecreative.com / info@lovecreative.com

James Lunn
www.memo-random.com / lunn360@hotmail.com

Maldesign (Andy Mallalieu)
www.maldesign.co.uk / andy@maldesign.co.uk

MARK Studio (Mark Lester)
www.markstudio.co.uk / mark@markstudio.co.uk

Claire McManus (Ampersand8)
www.ampersand8.co.uk / claire@ampersand8.co.uk

NB: Studio
www.nbstudio.co.uk / d.lock@nbstudio.co.uk

NODE Berlin Oslo
www.nodeberlin.com / mail@nodeberlin.com

Nth Creative
www.nthcreative.co.uk / tim@nthcreative.co.uk

ODD (Simon Glover)
www.thankodd.com / info@thankodd.com

Karin von Ompteda
info@inclusivetype.org

Oscar & Ewan (Oscar Bauer and Ewan Robertson)
www.oscarandewan.co.uk / mail@oscarandewan.co.uk

Akinori Oishi
aki-air.com / aki98@iamas.ac.jp

Pandarosa
www.pandarosa.net / info@pandarosa.net

Parent
www.parentdesign.co.uk / mail@parentdesign.co.uk

Peter and Paul
www.peterandpaul.co.uk / paul@peterandpaul.co.uk

pleaseletmedesign
www.pleaseletmedesign.com /
oh@pleaseletmedesign.com

Radford Wallis
www.radfordwallis.com / design@radfordwallis.com

Red Design
www.red-design.co.uk / info@red-design.co.uk

Tom Rowe (Evening Tweed)
www.eveningtweed.com/ hello@eveningtweed.com

Serge Seidlitz
www.sergeseidlitz.com / mail@sergeseidlitz.com

Studio8 Design
www.studio8design.co.uk / info@studio8design.co.uk

Studio Daniel Baer
www.danielbaer.co.uk / info@danielbaer.co.uk

Studio Oscar
www.studiooscar.com / info@studiooscar.com

Studio-SM (Sofia Leverbeck and Magnus Polbratt)
www.studio-sm.co.uk / hello@studio-sm.co.uk

Surface
www.surface.de / katrin@surface.de

Henrik Tandberg
henriktandberg@gmail.com

The Apartment
www.theapt.com / anne@theapt.com

TNOP™ DESIGN
www.tnop.com / tnop@tnop.com

Tom Brown Art+Design (TBA+D)
www.tbad.ca / t.brown@tbad.ca

Turnbull Grey
www.turnbullgrey.co.uk / info@turnbullgrey.co.uk

Turnstyle
www.turnstylestudio.com / info@turnstylestudio.com

Underline Studio
www.underlinestuio.com / info@underlinestudio.com

unfolded
unfolded.ch / we@unfolded.ch

Pierre Vanni
www.pierrevanni.com / pvanni@hotmail.fr

Ben Weeks
www.benweeks.ca / ben@benweeks.ca

Steven Wilson
wilson2000.com / steve@wilson2000.com

Acknowledgments

I'd like to thank all the designers around the world who took the time and effort to submit work for inclusion in this book. Of course, without your contributions, making this book would not have been possible. Special thanks also to Kate Bingaman-Burt, Clara Courtaigne, Ariel Aguilera, Andrea Benyi, Peter Crnokrak, Chris Turnbull, and Bruce Slorach. Thank-you to Simon Slater for the design, Simon Punter for the photography, and the continued support of the team at RotoVision.

This book is for Mum.

Index